Essential
Rome

by Jane Shaw

Jane Shaw grew up in Edinburgh and lived in
London for several years before fleeing to Rome
in the early 1990s, where she lives in the heart of
Trastevere, writing, editing and translating. She
has contributed to guide books to Rome and Italy
for Time Out, Dorling Kindersley and Insight,
among others.

Above: *the Pantheon, Piazza Rotonda*

AA Publishing

Above: *a Swiss Guard at the Vatican*

Written by Jane Shaw

First published in 1998
Reprinted Jun and Nov 1998; Jun 1999.
Reprinted 2001. Information verified and updated.
Reprinted Feb 2002

© 2001 Automobile Association Developments Limited
Maps © 2001 Automobile Association Developments Limited
Reprinted Aug 2002
Published by AA Publishing, a trading name of Automobile Association Developments Limited, whose registered office is Millstream, Maidenhead Road, Windsor SL4 5GD.
Registered number 1878835.

The Automobile Association retains the copyright in the original edition © 1998 and in all subsequent editions, reprints and amendments.

A CIP catalogue record for this book is available from the British Library.

ISBN 0 7495 1640 2

The contents of this publication are believed correct at the time of printing. Nevertheless, the publishers cannot be held responsible for any errors or omissions or for changes in the details given in this guide or for the consequences of any reliance on the information it provides. Assessments of attractions, hotels, restaurants and other sights are based upon the author's personal experience and, therefore, necessarily contain elements of subjective opinion which may not reflect the publisher's opinion or dictate a reader's own experience on another occasion.

We have tried to ensure accuracy in this guide, but things do change and we would be grateful if readers would advise us of any inaccuracies they may encounter.

Colour separation: BTB Digital Imaging, Whitchurch, Hampshire
Printed and bound in Italy by Printer Trento Srl

Contents

About this Book

KEY TO SYMBOLS

✚ map reference to the maps found in the What to See section (see below)

✉ address or location

☎ telephone number

🕐 opening times

🍴 restaurant or café on premises or near by

Ⓜ nearest underground train station

🚌 nearest bus/tram route

🚆 nearest overground train station

⛴ ferry crossings and excursions by boat

✈ travel by air

ℹ tourist information

♿ facilities for visitors with disabilities

✋ admission charge

↔ other places of interest near by

❓ other practical information

➤ indicates the page where you will find a fuller description

---

Essential *Rome* is divided into five sections to cover the most important aspects of your visit to Rome.

Viewing Rome pages 5–14
An introduction to Rome by the author.
  Rome's Features
  Essence of Rome
  The Shaping of Rome
  Peace and Quiet
  Rome's Famous

Top Ten pages 15–26
The author's choice of the Top Ten places to visit in Rome, each with practical information.

What to See pages 27–90
The two main areas of Rome, each with its own brief introduction and an alphabetical listing of the main attractions.
  Practical information
  Snippets of 'Did You Know…' information
  4 suggested walks
  2 suggested tours
  2 features

Where To... pages 91–116
Detailed listings of the best places to eat, stay, shop, take the children and be entertained.

4

Practical Matters pages 117–24
A highly visual section containing essential travel information.

Maps
All map references are to the individual maps found in the What to See section of this guide.
For example, Galleria Borghese has the reference ✚ 29D4 – indicating the page on which the map is located and the grid square in which the gallery is to be found. A list of the maps that have been used in this travel guide can be found in the index.

Prices
Where appropriate, an indication of the cost of an establishment is given by £ signs:
£££ denotes higher prices, ££ denotes average prices, while £ denotes lower charges.

Star Ratings
Most of the places described in this book have been given a separate rating:

✪✪✪   Do not miss
✪✪   Highly recommended
✪   Worth seeing

Viewing
Rome

Above: *Castel Sant'Angelo*
Right: *shopping by scooter*

5

Jane Shaw's Rome

Vatican City
Rome is the capital of the Roman Catholic church, for in it lies the Vatican City (Città del Vaticano), covering less than half a hectare, and really a separate state with its own post office, radio and TV stations. Rome abounds in nuns, monks and priests from all over the world who come to study at one of the Catholic universities; in and around St Peter's you can see an exotic array of the habits worn by various religious orders.

St Peter's is impressive even at dusk

Rome has got it all – a climate that gives sunny days at any time of year, a cuisine that has something (and usually a lot of things) for all tastes and some of the best fine art and architecture in the world. This is a city of contrasts; a bustling, modern capital set amid ancient splendour where screeching *motorini* swoop past leisurely pedestrians, classical art competes for attention with high fashion, and a beautiful sunny day can suddenly throw up a sky-blackening storm with thunder like cannon fire and rain that'll soak you in seconds.

It helps to approach it with a flexible attitude. You may not always be able to achieve what you set out to do (museums, shops, restaurants and even occasionally banks sometimes close suddenly for one reason or another), but don't worry. There are plenty of other things to do and even the streetlife, with its constantly changing parade of locals and visitors alike, is worth watching from a pavement or piazza bar. There are intriguing juxtapositions everywhere: in narrow winding streets of terracotta buildings clothes boutiques nestle among family-run grocers, craft studios, art galleries and restaurants.

The weather helps create a relaxed way of life in which even the most simple transaction may need far more time than you would have thought possible. On the other hand, lunch can take all afternoon so you'll probably soon stop worrying that the overseas post takes rather longer than expected. There is notorious bureaucracy and time-consuming public service (but these are improving), but once you adjust to the pace of life, you realise how much of Rome functions extremely efficiently, including the bus service, which gets you where you want in central Rome more or less when you want.

The beauty of Rome is a magnet to artists, tourists and students, many of whom never quite manage to leave it.

Rome's Features

Population

The city of Rome is roughly 2,700 years old. It has a population of over 3 million – up from 200,000 in 1870 when Italy became a unified nation (although there were well over 1 million people living in the city in the days of the empire). There are about 192,000 foreigners resident in Rome. About 10 million people arrive at Fiumicino airport every year. About two-thirds of the working population are in government administration; few work in industry – 100,000, while 600,000 people work in offices. The city covers about 1,500sq km and 12 hills, having expanded somewhat from the original seven hills of Rome.

Climate

The best seasons for visiting are April to June, September and October – also the busiest, although the real peak comes at Easter when pilgrims swell the crowds of tourists who descend on the city. The average annual temperature is 16°C with a high of 38°C and a low of -4°C.

Crime

The bag-snatching and pocket-picking sectors of the Roman criminal community pose the biggest threat to visitors. Here there is good news and bad. 1996 saw bag-snatches, called *scippi* and traditionally committed by masked figures on motor scooters, register a 6 per cent decrease on the year before, at 13,333. But there was a 3 per cent rise in picked pockets, at 85,245.

In July and August temperatures can reach 40°C and in August a lot of businesses close for the holidays. Early spring and late autumn are the wettest seasons (you can be unlucky at other times as well) – Rome has a similar annual rainfall to London but most falls over a few days. Even in winter the weather can be glorious with maximum daily temperatures around 15 or 16°C but, although it seldom snows, there can be bitingly cold winds in December, January and early February.

Carabinieri police watch the world go by in Piazza Venezia

Churches and Bars

Central Rome has over 400 churches, 600 bars and less than 40 public toilets (but do not panic, most bars will allow you to use theirs). There are also 150km of holes in the road.

Essence of Rome

Central Rome on both sides of the Tiber (Tevere) is a city of contrasts. This busy modern capital is squeezed into a maze of old streets in which the layers of more than 2,000 years of history are superimposed on each other: ancient columns embedded in Renaissance palaces, baroque façades slapped on to the front of Romanesque churches and 1930s fascist office buildings nestling among it all. Not only is Rome the seat of the Italian government (both the President and the Prime Minister have their official residences here), but it is also a world centre for the film and fashion industries.

Legend has it that Romulus and Remus were breast-fed by a wolf and founded Rome; the beautiful and busy Piazza Navona

THE **10** ESSENTIALS

If you only have a short time to visit Rome, or would like to get a really complete picture of the city, here are the essentials:

• **Go to the Vatican** and marvel at Michelangelo's masterpieces in the Sistine Chapel (▶ 24).

• **Look down on Rome from on high** (▶ 34 for suggested view points), and try to find the flattish dome

• **Walk the streets at the Forum** where Julius Caesar trod (▶ 22).

• **At St Peter's look on the floor of the central aisle** (▶ 26) where the lengths of other cathedrals' aisles are marked – see how your local one measures up.

• **Do the historic centre walk** (▶ 26) to take you past some of the most famous tourist sights in the world.

• **Try to imagine the Colosseum** (▶ 18) full of raucous crowds with wild animals and hapless humans fighting it out in the ring.

• **Throw a coin into the Trevi Fountain** (▶ 40) which guarantees your return. Italian currency ends up in the coffers of the town council; foreign coins are donated to the Red Cross.

with a hole in the middle, which is the Pantheon (▶ 20).

• **Find a bar on Piazza Navona** (▶ 21) or Campo de' Fiori (▶ 37), sip a drink and watch life saunter by.

• **See Rome by night,** preferably on foot. Many of the main monuments are floodlit and those that are not have an eerie beauty in the city's soft street lighting.

• **Visit the church of Santa Maria in Cosmedin** (▶ 68) to test your nerve with your hand in the *Bocca della Verità* (mouth of truth), which will bite if you tell a lie.

Illuminated Santa Maria in Trastevere creates an atmospheric meeting place; Piazza Navona's cafés are popular by day

9

The Shaping of Rome

753 BC
Rome founded by Romulus, the first of seven kings.

616–576 BC
Under Tarquin the Elder the Forum and Circo Massimo are established.

509 BC
Tarquin the Proud, last of the kings, expelled and Brutus establishes the Republic.

312 BC
Via Appia Antica started and Aqua Appia, the first aqueduct.

168 BC
Rome conquers Greece.

149–146 BC
Carthage destroyed in third Punic war.

60 BC
Julius Caesar, Crassus and Pompey form the Triumvirate.

51 BC
Conquest of Gaul.

44 BC
Murder of Julius Caesar.

27 BC
Augustus becomes the first emperor.

AD 64
Fire destroys much of the city (Emperor Nero plays his fiddle).

AD 67
Crucifixion of St Peter and execution of St Paul during first persecution of Christians.

312
Battle of Milvian bridge, Constantine wins control of the Empire.

380
Christianity becomes the Roman Empire's official religion.

395
Empire divided into two parts, Eastern and Western.

410
Rome sacked by Goths.

455
Rome sacked by Vandals.

475
Fall of Western Roman Empire.

778
Charlemagne conquers Italy.

961
King Otto of the Saxons becomes first Holy Roman Emperor.

1300
First Holy Year proclaimed by Pope Boniface VIII.

1309
Pope Clement V moves papacy to Avignon

1347
Cola di Rienzo tries to establish a new Roman Republic.

1377
Papacy returns from Avignon.

1378
Great Schism in papacy, a second 'pope' is established in Avignon.

1409
A third papacy established in Pisa.

1417
Pope Martin V ends the Great Schism.

1453
Fall of Constantinople to the Turks, marking end of Eastern Empire.

1498–1502
Papacy at war with Italian states.

1506
Work starts on new St Peter's.

1508–1512
Papacy at war with Romagna.

1520
Martin Luther's reforming thesis starts the Reformation.

1527
Rome sacked by Charles V and German and Spanish troops.

An impression of the Tiber in ancient times

1929
Lateran Treaty between Mussolini and the papacy creates Vatican state.

1940
Italy enters World War II.

1943
Mussolini resigns and Germans take over.

1944
Allies liberate Rome from Germans.

1946
Republic established, King Umberto II exiled.

1957
Treaty of Rome establishes Common Market (now European Union).

1960
Olympic games held in Rome.

1978
Prime Minister Aldo Moro assassinated.

1981
Pope John Paul II shot in St Peter's square.

1993
Anti-corruption movement starts in Italy; two bombs explode – at San Giovanni in Laterano and at San Giorgio in Velabro. Mafia blamed.

2000
Many millions of pilgrims descend on Rome for the Holy Year.

1545–63
Council of Trent leads to the Counter Reformation to strengthen the Catholic church against reforming Protestants.

1585
Pope Sixtus V plans new city with many new streets and buildings.

1600
Giordano Bruno burned at the stake in Campo de' Fiori.

1626
New St Peter's consecrated.

1797
Napoleon captures Rome.

1801
Concordat between Napoleon and Pope Pius VII.

1806
Holy Roman Empire ends.

1808
Rome occupied by French; Pius VII sent to France in captivity.

1814
Pius VII returns to Rome.

1820
Wars for Italian Unification begin.

1849–66
French troops in Rome protect the Pope from the armies of Unification.

1861
Kingdom of Italy formed under King Vittorio Emanuele.

1870
Rome captured by General Garibaldi's troops; Italian Unification complete.

1922
Mussolini marches on Rome, becomes Prime Minister.

Peace & Quiet

Rome is not a quiet city. Heavy traffic and vast numbers of tourists combine to make sightseeing a tiring, sometimes stressful, business, particularly in the spring, early summer and autumn. But do not despair, even in the packed historic centre it is possible to come across havens of peace – a little piazza or quiet alley – where you can sit for a moment or two. Some of the sights themselves are often relatively tranquil. The Palatino, Piazza Farnese, the Terme di Caracalla and Circo Massimo, for example, are usually fairly empty, and on the hill above Circo Massimo the town's rose garden will refresh your senses and restore your energy levels.

Parks and Gardens

There are a number of parks and gardens in or near the city centre. The most central of these is Villa Borghese which stretches out behind the Pincio Gardens above Piazza del Popolo (➤ 59). Here there are lakes, flower gardens, trees and rolling hillsides on which to rest. Above the Colosseum is the Colle Oppio, a slightly run-down turn-of-the-century style park which contains the ruins of Nero's Golden House and Trajan's baths as well as some inviting benches. On the other side of the Colosseum is the park of Villa Celimontana (entrance on Piazza della Navicella) laid out as formal gardens for the Mattei family in the 16th century. Off Via di Santa Sabina on the Aventine hill there's the Parco di San Alessio and a most delightful orangery with good views over Trastevere. In Trastevere itself you will find the botanical gardens (on Via Corsini off Via della Lungara), pretty Villa Sciarra (entrance on Via Calandrelli) built on a steep hillside and the massive Villa Doria Pamphili (entrance on Via di San Pancrazio) with its statues, trees, fountains and artificial river.

One of the ancient bridges linking Isola Tiberina to the river bank

Wild Cats
Although not exactly wild, Rome is famous for its cats, many of whom live in the streets or among the ruins relying on the goodwill of local people, or informal cat protection organisations, to feed them. The recent increase in these charitable souls may have something to do with the increasing boldness of some of the local rats (although don't worry, you are no more likely to come across a rat than you are in any other major city).

Roman Wildlife

The crumbling masonry of ancient Rome contains a wide array of plants, small animals and birds. In the 19th century, for example, several specific studies of

the flora of the Colosseum were made and hundreds of plant species were identified. Many of these have since disappeared but in spring there is still a flamboyant display of wild and semi-wild flowers sprouting up in the Fori Imperiali (▶ 40). If you look carefully, you may catch sight of little birds or scuttling lizards, particularly the green-grey Sicilian lizard or even the far rarer green lizard. Geckos, on the other hand, are everywhere. The more exotic birdlife includes the blue rock thrush, the black redstart, little owls and kestrels.

The most famous of the city's trees are the pines of Rome, the aptly named umbrella pine (*Pinus pinea*). Many of the palm trees were planted at the end of the 19th century while orange trees, which sometimes drop their soggy fruit at the feet of passers-by, have long been used to decorate palace and convent gardens.

Finally, a word of warning for hayfever sufferers: the plane trees that line the river and some of the main streets emit a particularly potent pollen in spring.

National Park

Those who want to get right away from the city head off to the Parco Nazionale d'Abruzzo, 400sq km of alpine scenery which includes some of the highest peaks in the Apennine range (2,000m and above) and a network of well sign-posted walking, rambling and hiking routes. The park boasts a spectacular range of (admittedly rather shy) animals and birds including bears, wolves, chamonix, lynx, wild boars (which also feature on some local menus), eagles, falcons and owls. The centre of the park is Pescasseroli reached by bus from Via Tiburtina or car by way of Licenza or Subiaco.

Peaceful today; Circo Massimo was once the site of chariot races and blood sports

Rome's Famous

St Peter was martyred here in AD 67

As the former capital of the Roman Empire, the headquarters of the Roman Catholic church and the capital of modern Italy, it is hardly surprising that Rome has attracted a vast array of talented and important people from all professions.

One former resident who went on to true greatness, as guardian of the gates of Heaven, was St Peter. Christ's disciple came to Rome around AD 42. He was one of the first Christian martyrs and was crucified (upside down as he felt unworthy of dying as Christ had) in AD 67 under Emperor Nero.

Artists

The artists who came to Rome include Michelangelo (1475–1564) who was here from 1506. This tempestuous, troubled genius is believed to have been homosexual and always used male models, even when representing women. In contrast, Raphael (1483–1520) who came to Rome in 1508, fell in love with one of his models – the *Fornarina* (baker's daughter) (► 19). Caravaggio (1571–1610) was in Rome from 1591 until he had to flee justice in 1606 after killing his tennis opponent in a fight.

Monarchs

Among the monarchs who sought refuge was Queen Christina of Sweden (1626–89) who was welcomed by the Pope after her conversion to Catholicism. In 1715 another Catholic royal, James Edward Stuart (1688–1766), fled here after his unsuccessful attempt to win back the British throne for his family. His son, Charles Edward (Bonnie Prince Charlie), was born here in 1721 and died at Palazzo Balestra near Piazza Venezia in 1788.

Napoleon

Napoleon Bonaparte arrived in Rome at the head of his conquering army in 1797. After his defeat and death in 1821 his family continued to live here.

Writers

Visiting writers include Johann Wolfgang Goethe (1749–1832) who lived on Via del Corso from 1786 to 1788. Henry James (1843–1916) was a frequent visitor, while the English 19th-century poets Keats, Shelley, Byron, Robert Browning and Elizabeth Barrett-Browning all knew the city well. Author Alberto Moravia (1907–90) was born in Rome; many of his novels and stories are set here.

Film Directors

Two of the most famous film-makers of the 20th century set some of their best works in Rome and are still fondly remembered by those who knew them. Federico Fellini's (1920–93) *La Dolce Vita* became synonymous with Rome in the 1960s, especially the scene where Marcello Mastroianni follows Anita Ekberg into the Fontana di Trevi. Pier Paolo Pasolini (1922–75) used a mixture of contemporary and historic settings for his erudite films. He was brutally murdered in 1975 on the coast near Rome.

Top Ten

Above: *The Colosseum*
Right: *Angel, Ponte Sant'Angelo*

1
Campidoglio

🕂 28C2

✉ Piazza del Campidoglio

☎ 06 6710 2071/
6710 2475

🕐 Tue–Sat 9–7, Sun
9–1:30

🚌 44, 46, 75, 81, 95, 160,
170, 175, 181, 719 to
Piazza Venezia

♿ None

✋ Moderate; free last Sun
of each month

*Piazza del Campidoglio is
home to the art and
sculpture collections of
the Capitoline Museums*

*The Capitoline Museums house one of Europe's
most impressive collections of ancient sculpture –
started by the popes in the 15th century.*

Michelangelo designed Rome's magnificent civic centre,
although later architects finished the job. Today, only the
salmon-pink Palazzo Senatorio is used for political
purposes (the mayor's office is here), while the flanking
buildings form the Campidoglio (or Capitoline) Museums.

On entering the Palazzo Nuovo, on the left, you are
greeted by the enormous 2nd-century AD bronze equestrian statue of Emperor Marcus Aurelius which rested atop
the pedestal in the centre of the square until 1981. On the
first floor in room 1 (Sala 1), is a superbly modelled,
sensual *Dying Gaul*; like many sculptures here, this is a
Roman copy in marble of an earlier Greek work. Roman
heads abound, including portraits of philosophers (a whole
roomful) and eminent citizens with elaborate hair. The
erotic *Capitoline Venus* has a chamber to herself.

In the courtyard of the Palazzo dei Conservatori
opposite are giant hands, a head and feet – fragments
from a colossal statue of
Constantine found in the Forum.
Upstairs, highlights include the
creamy marble *Venus Esquilina*
and the delightfully realistic 1st
century BC bronze *Spinario*, a
young boy extracting a thorn
from his foot. The *She-Wolf
Suckling Romulus and Remus* in
the Sala della Lupa will be
familiar to many – the symbol of
Rome is reproduced every-
where. The wolf is thought to be
an Etruscan bronze of the late
6th to early 5th centuries BC to
which the twins were added in
the 16th century.

The picture gallery on the
second floor provides no relief
for the footsore. There are fine
works by Pietro da Cortona,
Guido Reni, Tintoretto, Rubens,
Van Dyck, and others; Caravaggio's sensual *St John the
Baptist* in his fully-fledged realist
style and Guercino's immense
Burial of St Petronilla stand out.

2
Castel Sant'Angelo

This powerful monument on the Tiber symbolises almost 2,000 years of Roman history, from Hadrian to Italian Unification.

Castel Sant'Angelo was central to the history of the papacy and the defence of the city until 1886 when it was turned into a museum. It is a labyrinth of a place both literally and historically.

Built by Emperor Hadrian (AD 117–138) as a mausoleum to himself, visitors today enter via the original Roman passageway, up which the funeral procession passed. This joins up with one of the medieval ramps that were added when the tomb was converted into a defensive fortress. The dark ramp finally opens on to a courtyard (originally the funerary garden), where now there is Montelupo's statue of an angel (1544) sheathing a sword, commemorating (along with the monument's name) a legendary event in which an angel was seen over Rome at the end of a plague in 590.

Off the courtyard (with its Michelangelo façade from 1514) is the *Sala di Apollo* (1548), exquisitely decorated with ornate *grotteschi* (frescoes); illuminated windows in the floor give you a view down to the underground corridors that led to a notorious papal prison. Following Medici Pope Clement VII's seven-month siege inside the *Castello* (1527), the popes felt they needed more sumptuous apartments. Farnese Pope Paul III (1534–49) commissioned the magnificent *Sala Paolina*, with its beautiful frescoes and *trompe l'oeil* doors. Off the library (with gorgeous stucco work) is the wood-lined papal treasury, the room believed to have held Hadrian's tomb, although the whereabouts of his remains are a mystery. The tour finishes with a walk around the ramparts.

➕ 28B4

✉ Lungotevere Castello 50

☎ 06 681 9111

🕐 Tue–Sun 9–7

🍴 Bar on ramparts (£££)

Ⓜ Lepanto

🚌 49, 70, 87, 280, 492, 926 to Piazza Cavour

✋ Moderate

Castel Sant' Angelo has been mausoleum, fortress, papal prison and museum

17

3
Colosseum (Colosseo)

✝ 29D2

✉ Piazza del Colosseo

☎ 06 700 4261

🕐 Tue–Sat 9 to 1 hour before sunset; Sun, Mon 9–2

Ⓜ Colosseo

🚌 75, 81, 85, 87, 175, 673 to Piazza del Colosseo

♿ Very few

✋ Moderate

❓ Pope leads the stations of the cross here on the evening of Good Friday

The Colosseum takes its name from the Colossus of Nero, a huge bronze statue which once stood close by

Built in the 1st century AD as a gift to the Romans, this dignified, round monument has become the city's most recognisable symbol.

Emperor Vespasian commissioned the Colosseum to fill the site of a massive lake that his predecessor, Nero, had had excavated for his own private use. The massive circus, with a capacity of more than 55,000, was used for popular, bloodthirsty spectator sports. In spite of centuries of use as an unofficial marble quarry for Renaissance and baroque builders, much of the outer shell has survived showing the four arched tiers (each arch held a statue) behind which staircases and galleries led to the auditorium. Seating was segregated according to sex and status; the emperor's box was at the southern end (opposite today's main entrance) and below him sat the Vestal Virgins.

Nearly all the events staged here guaranteed the bloody death of human participants. Gladiators were usually slaves, prisoners of war or condemned prisoners but the enthusiastic following that a successful gladiator provoked encouraged some upper-class men to train for combat. Other spectacles involved mismatched rivals fighting to the death with nets, tridents and other weapons; fights against wild animals were also popular. The labyrinth of underground passages, lifts and cages through which these unfortunate beasts were channelled into the ring can be seen under the arena. Gladiatorial combat was banned in the 5th century, and changing public tastes led to the Colosseum falling out of use by the 6th century.

4
Palazzo Barberini

*A treasure trove of paintings from the 13th
to the 16th centuries is housed in one of Rome's
grandest baroque palaces.*

Carlo Maderno's original design, begun in 1624 for
Barberini Pope Urban VIII, was embellished by Bernini and
Maderno's nephew Borromini. The latter added the
elegant oval staircase and the windows of the upper
storey which, using ingenious artificial perspective,
preserve the symmetry of the façade while staying in
proportion with the size of the actual rooms.

The palace was sold to the Italian state in 1949 and
houses, together with Palazzo Corsini (➤ 53), the national

*The palace itself is as
beautiful as the art it
houses*

collection of art. There are plans to remove the officers'
mess which occupies a large area, expand the gallery and
reunite the collection. In the meantime extensive renovations are bringing the main rooms back to their original
splendour, the most spectacular of which is the *Gran
Salone*, with its elaborate ceiling fresco, *Triumph of Divine
Providence*, by Pietro da Cortona.

Magnificent *quattrocento* panel paintings include an
ethereal *Annunciation* by Filippo Lippi, and a *Madonna and
Saints* by Alunno. The highlights of the collection are the
16th- and 17th-century paintings: Andrea del Sarto's
magical *Sacra Famiglia*; Raphael's *La Fornarina* (widely
believed to be a portrait of the baker's daughter who was
his mistress, although some maintain it is in fact a picture
of a courtesan and was painted by Giulio Romano); a
portrait of Urban VIII by Bernini (his genius lay more in
sculpture and architecture); and works by El Greco,
Bronzino, Guido Reni, Guercino and Caravaggio.

 29D4

 Via Quattro Fontane 13

06 481 4591/482 4184

 Tue–Sun 9–7

 Metro Barberini

 60, 61, 62, 175, 492,
590 to Piazza Barberini;
590 has facilities for
passengers with
reduced mobility

 None

 Moderate

5
Pantheon

*Its massive circular interior, lit only
by a round opening in the roof, is one of the most
awe-inspiring sights of Rome.*

*The incredible dome of
the Pantheon*

 28C3

 Piazza della Rotonda

06 6830 0230

Mon–Sat 9–6:30, Sun 9–1

119 to Piazza della
Rotonda; 44, 64, 70, 75,
81 to Largo di Torre
Argentina

 Few

 Free

Sometimes used for
concerts and special
services

Do not be misled by the inscription, *AGRIPPA FECIT*, over its portals. Agrippa built an earlier version of this temple to all the gods but what we see today was erected by Emperor Hadrian in the early 1st century AD and, in spite of losing many of its opulent trimmings over the centuries, it remains much as he would have remembered it.

The dome is a semi-sphere 43.5m in diameter with walls 6m thick, it was constructed by pouring concrete over a wooden framework. Originally the roof was covered with bronze cladding which was stripped off by Constantine II in the 7th century to decorate Constantinople and, 1,000 years later, Bernini took the remaining bronze from the roof beams to build the canopy (*baldacchino*) in St Peter's (► 26). Its huge bronze doors, however, have survived since Roman times. The ornate marble floor is a 19th-century reconstruction of the original design and the interior has been cleaned and touched up to restore its subtly vibrant colours.

It was one of the first Roman temples to be converted into a church (by Pope Boniface IV when Emperor Phocas donated the building to him; consecrated 609) and over the centuries several leading Italians, including the painter Raphael, have been buried here.

6
Piazza Navona

One of the world's most beautiful squares owes its elongated shape to the ancient Roman stadium over which it was built.

Although the best effect can be had by approaching Piazza Navona from the southeast end, whichever of the narrow streets you take, this massive space in the cramped historical centre is always breathtaking. To its north, are remains of the entrance to the stadium that Emperor Domitian built in the 1st century AD.

The piazza's centrepiece is Bernini's spectacular Fontana dei Fiumi (fountain of the rivers, 1651) featuring symbolic representations of the rivers Ganges, Danube, Plate and Nile (blindfolded because its source was then unknown) clinging to a massive artificial cliff-face while sea monsters lurk beneath. The figure at the centre of the fountain to the southeast is another Bernini work, *Il Moro* (the moor); the figures of Neptune and others on the third fountain are 19th-century.

This has always been a hub of Roman social life; there was a market here for centuries and the piazza used to be flooded in August to form a vast watery playground for rich and poor alike. Today it is flooded by musicians, artists, locals and visitors who flock to its bars for hours at a time.

 28B3

Piazza Navona

Lots of bars, tend to be expensive but worth it (££)

46, 62, 64 to Corso Vittorio Emanuele II; 70, 81, 87, 115, 186, 492, 628 to Corso del Rinascimento

December Christmas fair (▶ 116), street performers all year

Bernini's fountain, topped by an obelisk, reigns over Piazza Navona

7
Roman Forum (Foro Romano)

🕂 28C3

✉ Via dei Fori Imperiali

☎ 06 699 0110

🕐 Apr–Sep, Mon 9–2,
Tue–Sat 9 to sunset;
Oct–Mar, Mon–Sat 9–3,
Sun 9–1

*Survey the monumental
ruins of Classical Rome*

*This was the social, economic and political centre
of ancient Rome, where people came to shop,
consult lawyers or gossip.*

Before entering the Foro or Forum, look down on it from
behind the Campidoglio (► 16). To your left is the Arch of
Septimius Severus, erected in AD 203 to celebrate his
victory over the Parthians; behind it, to the right, is the
Column of Phocas, AD 608, erected in honour of the
Byzantine Emperor, Phocas, in gratitude after he gave the
Pantheon (► 20) to the Pope.

🚇 Colosseo

🚌 85, 87, 175, 186 to Via
dei Fori Imperiali; 81 to
Piazza del Colosseo; 44,
46, 60, 81, 94, 95, 710,
719 to Piazza Venezia

♿ Few

✋ Moderate (includes
entrance to Palatino,
► 52)

❓ Guided tours available;
booking ☎ 06 3908
0730

Left of the public entrance to the Forum is the Basilica
Aemilia, a place for business; look for traces of the coins
that were fused into the floor when the Basilica was
burned down in the 5th century. Next to the Basilica, along
the Via Sacra (Sacred Way), is the 3rd-century Curia (rebuilt
in the 1930s) where the Senate met; the slightly curved
platform outside it is the rostrum on which political
speeches and orations were made. Opposite the Curia is
the 1st-century BC Basilica Julia and to its left is the
Temple of Castor and Pollux, with its three beautiful
remaining columns. The round building is the Temple of
Vesta, where a fire was kept burning continually by the 16
Vestal Virgins who lived in the elegant villa behind it. On
the other side of the Forum are the three massive vaults of
the 4th-century Basilica of Maxentius and Constantine
much studied by Renaissance artists and architects. To its
left is the 4th-century AD Temple of Romulus, under which
you can see some dank little rooms, thought to be the
remains of a much earlier brothel. The Arch of Titus is near
the public exit; it was erected in the 1st century AD to
celebrate the Emperor's sack of Jerusalem.

8
San Clemente

*A 12th-century church, on top of a 4th-century one,
on top of an ancient shrine of Mithras – a walk
through Rome's multi-layered history?*

Even without its hidden depths, San Clemente is one of
the prettiest churches in Rome with its 12th-century apse
mosaic, *The Triumph of the Cross*, showing details of
animals, birds and humans in flower-filled fields and its
simple, 6th-century choir stall, originally in the earlier
church building. The spiralling column next to the choir stall
is a 12th-century cosmati (► 68) mosaic candlestick. To
the left of the entrance is the chapel of St Catherine with
15th-century frescoes by Masolini of her life and
martyrdom on the original Catherine-wheel.

However, the church's main claim to fame lies underneath where the first layer comprises the remains of a
4th-century church in which some fragments of ancient
masonry and 11th-century frescoes, illustrating the life
and miracles of St Clemente (martyred by being tied to
an anchor and drowned), have been preserved among
the foundations of the later church. There is also a
large circular well that was
probably used as a font.

Descending yet further
you come to the ancient
Roman level where the
highlight is a cramped room
with a small altar on which
there is a relief of Mithras
slaying a bull. The Mithraic
cult arrived in Rome from
Persia about the same time
as Christianity and had a
strong following especially
among soldiers (women
were not allowed to join),
involving them in ritualistic
banquets.

The route out takes you
through the walls of several
ancient Roman apartment
blocks and even lower,
although not open to the
public, are some 5th or 6th
century catacombs.

*View of San Clemente's
attractive main façade*

🕂 29D2

✉ Via di San Giovanni in
Laterano

☎ 06 7045 1018

🕐 9–12:30, 3:30–6:30;
Oct–Mar closes at 6

Ⓜ Colosseo

🚌 85 to Via di San
Giovanni in Laterano;
87, 186 to Via Labicana

✋ Cheap; free to upper
church

9
Sistine Chapel & Vatican Museums

🕇 73B1

✉ Viale Vaticano

☎ Vatican tourist office: 06
6988 4947/6988 3333

🕒 Easter to mid-Jun,
Mon–Fri 8:45–4:45, Sat
8:45–1:45. Rest of year,
Mon–Sat 8:45–1:45. All
year, last Sun of month
8:45–1:45PM

🍴 Choice of restaurants
and bars (£)

Michelangelo's masterpiece is one of today's wonders of the world, fittingly reached via the rooms of one of the world's greatest art collections.

Before reaching the Sistine Chapel you will have to walk for about 20 minutes through the corridors of the Vatican Museums. There is far too much to be absorbed in one visit, but you can select one of several recommended timed routes to see a selection of the highlights. There are: the Museo Gregoriano-Egizio Egyptian collection; the Museo Chiaramonti collection of Roman sculpture; the Museo Pio Clementine, whose classical sculptures include the *Belvedere Apollo* and *Lacoön* and his sons being strangled by snakes; the Museo Gregoriano-Etrusco collection of Greek, Roman and Etruscan art; corridors of tapestries by Pieter van Aelst based on Raphael cartoons; and corridors lined with 16th-century maps of each of the Italian regions, which lead to the Raphael Rooms.

There are four Raphael Rooms, painted between 1508 and 1525 (the last finished by Giulio Romano after Raphael's death in 1520). In the first room the subjects are metaphysical, including the famous *School of Athens* in which many of Raphael's contemporaries are portrayed as Greek philosophers and poets. The second room shows biblical and early Christian events. The third room portrays significant events in papal history, and the final room illustrates the story of Constantine. From here the tour proceeds to the Sistine Chapel.

Michelangelo painted the Sistine Chapel ceiling between 1508 and 1512, crouching for hours on the scaffolding as Pope Julius II chivvied him on from below. A thorough cleaning in the 1980s and 1990s, during which some of the garments that more puritanical popes had had painted on to Michelangelo's scantily clad biblical figures were stripped off along with the dust and grime, restored the original vibrant colours. The ceiling tells the story of the Creation, in which a pink-clad God nips around dividing light from darkness and water from land before going on to create the

Above: *a detail from, and (right), the complete Michelangelo masterpiece,* The Last Judgement

sun, the moon, Adam and Eve. The last four panels show the birth of original sin and the story of Noah. On the chapel's end wall is Michelangelo's much later *Last Judgement*. By the time he started this in 1534 he was racked with ill-health and pessimistic thoughts of his own mortality, and it took him until 1541 to complete. The flayed skin held up by St Bartholomew (to Christ's left) is believed to be a self-portrait, while the diabolical figure in the bottom right-hand corner is a portrait of the Pope's secretary, who disapproved of Michelangelo's naturalistic handling of this sacred subject. The other walls of the chapel were painted with episodes from the lives of Christ and Moses by, among others, Botticelli, and Perugino.

Beyond the chapel are: the Vatican library with over one million valuable volumes, many dating from the Middle Ages; a gallery of modern religious art including works by Klee, Munch and Picasso; and collections of pagan and early Christian antiquities. It is definitely worth going into the *Pinacoteca* (picture gallery) which has a marvellous collection of medieval, Renaissance and baroque art including masterpieces by most of the most famous names in European art of the periods.

Ottaviano

23, 49, 81, 492, 907, 991 to Piazza del Risorgimento

Good

Expensive but it covers a lot; free last Sun of month

Guided tours available in a number of languages

10
St Peter's (San Pietro)

🕇 73B1

✉ Piazza San Pietro

☎ Vatican tourist office: 06 6988 4947/6988 3333

🌐 Apr–Oct, 7–7; Nov–Mar, 7–6

Ⓜ Ottaviano

🚌 62, 64 to Piazza San Pietro; 49, 81, 492, 907, 991 to Piazza del Risorgimento

✋ Free to Basilica; moderate for roof

❓ Tours of the necropolis in English must be booked in advance through the Uffizio degli Scavi in St Peter's Square. Papal blessing every Wed morning (unless he is away, as in Jun–Sep) and on Easter and Christmas days.

Looking down from the dome designed by Michelangelo

Whether you find its opulence impressive or over the top, the sheer size of the world's most important church will not leave you unmoved

Emperor Constantine built a shrine to St Peter over his tomb and near where he had been crucified in the Circus of Nero. As the fortunes of Rome and the newly established Christian religion rose and fell, the building saw periods of embellishment fluctuating with sackings and destruction, and had been much altered by the time Pope Nicholas V ordered its restoration in the mid-15th century. Work did not get under way until about 50 years later, however, when Pope Julius II appointed Bramante as the architect for a completely new basilica in 1503. Another 123 years, and interventions from many of the most important architects and artists of the time, were to pass before the new basilica was consecrated. The basic floor plan is more or less as Bramante designed it, 187m long; Michelangelo designed the 132.5m-high dome, Carlo Maderno the façade and Bernini the impressive oval colonnade that surrounds the piazza in front of the basilica.

Inside, on the right, is Michelangelo's *Pietà* of 1499. Other gems include a 13th-century bronze statue of St Peter whose foot has been worn away by the touch of pilgrims; Bernini's massive 20m-high *baldacchino*, or altar canopy (under which only the Pope can celebrate Mass), his monuments to Popes Urban VIII and Alexander VII and the tabernacle in the shape of a temple.

What To See

Above: *dome of St Peter's Basilica*
Right: *detail from the Sistine Chapel ceiling*

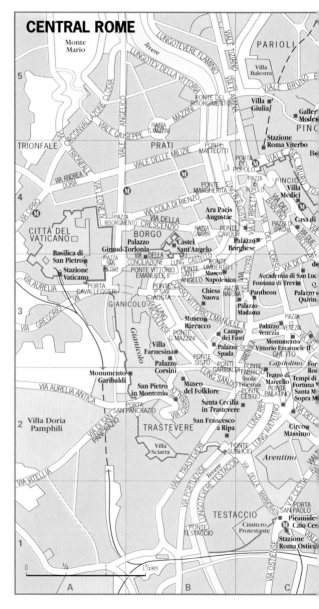

Rome

Rome has been a major city for longer than most other European capitals have existed. First the centre of the Roman Empire, a few centuries later it emerged as the centre of the Roman Catholic faith and finally, in 1870, it became the capital of the newly united Italy. In Rome's museums you can see artworks and artefacts from well over 2,000 years of history – exquisite ancient sculptures, delicate early Renaissance and opulent baroque paintings and much more. Sightseers' Rome breaks into two sections, ancient and Renaissance-baroque, but wherever you are you're likely to suddenly come across some remnant from centuries earlier than its surroundings.

Add the plethora of cool bars, ice-cream shops and restaurants as well as boutiques that attract the fashion-conscious and you've got a place that can guarantee a wonderful visit.

'At each step, a palace, a ruin, a garden, a desert, a little house, a stable, a triumphal arch, a colonnade, and all these so close together that one could draw them on a small sheet of paper.'

J W VON GOETHE
The Italian Journey (1786–8)

The City of Rome

Rome is an ideal city for sightseeing. Nearly all of the main monuments, museums and churches are within walking distance of each other and wherever you look, you are likely to come across some picturesque detail (flower-filled balconies, pristine shirts and sheets hanging out to dry, sleepy cats snoozing on car bonnets, ruined splendour, a little shrine with a portrait of the Madonna and perhaps even a candle) that is guaranteed to charm anybody used to more severe northern cities.

Mornings are the best times for catching opening hours; most churches and museums close at lunchtime and some, but by no means all, reopen at about 4 or 5PM. In summer the middle of the day tends to be too hot for sightseeing anyway so you can use this time for a rest or a leisurely lunch under the awnings of an outdoor restaurant.

The Vatican City, here viewed from across the Tiber, is the world's smallest independent sovereign state, and also the most ancient

What to See in Rome

ACCADEMIA DI SAN LUCA ✪

Rome's academy of fine arts was founded by Pope Gregory XIII in 1577. It moved to its present site, the Palazzo Carpegna, in the 1930s when its previous home was cleared to make way for Via dei Fori Imperiali. The building has an unusual inclined spiral ramp (designed by Borromini), instead of stairs, to the upper levels. The collection is predominantly the work of academicians, or was presented by them, with plenty of fine portraits and still lifes. Highlights include a fresco fragment by Raphael, three works attributed to Titian, and paintings by Guido Reni, Van Dyck and Angelica Kauffman, one of the few women members of the academy.

🕂 28C3
✉ Piazza dell'Accademia di San Luca 77
☎ 06 679 8850
🕐 Mon, Wed, Fri, last Sun of month 10–1
🚇 Barberini
🚌 52, 53, 56, 58, 60, 62, 71, 95, 115, 175, 492, 590 to Via del Tritone
♿ Few
👜 Free

ANTIQUARIO COMUNALE ✪

Set in a villa on the Celio hill, one of the seven hills of Rome, this small archaeological museum houses delightful artefacts of the area, many of which were unearthed at the end of the 19th century when the city was undergoing expansion. While the grander discoveries found their way into the more important national collections, the exhibits here include more mundane (but therefore perhaps more fascinating) everyday objects: kitchen equipment, tools and other domestic items, including a jointed doll from the 2nd century AD which was found in the tomb of a young girl.

🕂 29D2
✉ Viale del Parco del Celio 22
☎ 06 700 1569
🕐 Tue–Sat 9–6:30, Sun & hols 9–1. Closed Mon
🚇 Circo Massimo, Colosseo
🚌 81, 175 to Via Celio Vibenna; tram 13, 30B to Viale del Parco del Celio
👜 Cheap

ARA PACIS AUGUSTAE ✪✪

A modern glass pavilion on the banks of the Tiber houses

🕂 28C4
✉ Via di Ripeta
☎ 06 3600 3471
🕐 Tue–Sat 9–7, Sun 9–1
🚌 81, 115, 119, 125, 590, 913, 926 to Piazza Augusto Imperatore
♿ None
👜 Cheap

some of the finest Roman sculpture to have survived. The Ara Pacis (altar of peace) was commissioned by the Senate in 13 BC to celebrate the victories of Emperor Augustus in Spain and Gaul; the outer walls of the enclosure that surrounds it depict a procession in which the faces of the imperial family and other important Romans can be seen. The panels by the entrances represent some symbolic moments from the history and mythology of Rome. Behind the altar is the round mausoleum of Augustus, built by the forward-planning emperor in 28 BC, 42 years before his death.

A marble relief depicting the earth goddess Tellus with animals at her feet

ARCO DI COSTANTINO ★★

Although known as Constantine's Arch, scholars now believe that this magnificent monument outside the Colosseum was originally built in honour of the emperor, Trajan, and adopted by Constantine who made a few alterations and rededicated it to his own triumph over co-emperor Maxentius in AD 315. In any event, many of the carved panels and medallions were scavenged from older monuments, including the figures of Dacian prisoners at the top of the columns, which were almost certainly carved for Trajan.

29D2
Piazza del Colosseo
Colosseo
81, 175, 673 to Piazza del Colosseo
Free

BASILICA DI SAN GIOVANNI E PAOLO ★★

Archaeology meets legend in this church, built over a two-storey Roman house, and containing Roman and medieval frescoes (seen by appointment only). Saints John and Paul were martyred here in 362, and their bodies, discovered only in the 20th century, are now in an ancient porphyry urn under the altar. The inside was modelled in 1718. There is a 13th-century fresco in a small room near the altar which depicts Christ and his Apostles. The church itself is predominantly Byzantine and has one of the most beautiful belltowers in Rome (1150), which was added by the only English pope, Nicholas Breakspeake (Adrian IV) as well as a majestic portico incorporating ancient columns.

29D3
Daily 8–11:30, 3:30–5:30
Piazza dei Santi Giovanni e Paolo
Colosseo
81, 673 to Via della Navicella

Arco di Costantino, like most monuments in Rome, is built in travertine, a white stone from Tivoli

In the Know

If you only have a short time to visit Rome, or would like to get a real flavour of the city, here are some ideas:

10
Ways To Be A Local

Learn a few phrases in Italian for a wonderfully appreciative response.
Be an assertive pedestrian; Roman drivers may look like maniacs but they can have lightning quick reactions and stop if you look determined to cross the road. Make sure you choose a spot where drivers will see you in time, however, and do not take any chances.
Dress comfortably but not scruffily; whether you like the style or not, Italians are nearly always well turned out.
Women, do not be offended by what you may see as invasive male attention – be politely assertive if you do not reciprocate the interest.
Relax; walk at a dignified, leisurely pace. Never rush.
Try not to drink cappuccino after dinner.

Eat ice-cream in the street, but nothing else.
Jaywalk; never use pavements when you can stroll down the middle of the cobbled street.
Do not get drunk. Italians seldom do.

10
Top Places To Have Lunch

Binario 4 (➤ 93).
Cecilia Metella (➤ 93).
Enoteca Corsi (➤ 94).
Frontoni (£) Viale Trastevere 52–8 ☎ 06 581 2436. A massive range of fillings from which to invent your own pizza.
Insalata Ricca (£) Piazza di Pasquino 72, and Largo dei Chiavari 8 ☎ 06 6880 3656. Light pasta dishes and big, meal-in-themselves salads.
Lorodinapoli (➤ 95).
Panattoni (➤ 96).
Sora Margherita (➤ 98).
Volpetti (£) Via della Scrofa 31 ☎ 06 686 1940. *Tavola calda* plus snacky things to eat on

your feet or carry to the cavernous basement sitting area.
La Zucca Magica (➤ 99).

5
Best Views

- Gianicolo (➤ 43).
- Palatino (➤ 52).
- Pincio, Villa Borghese (➤ 12).
- Ponte Garibaldi
- St Peter's roof (➤ 26).

10
Top Activities

Explore: hire a *motorino* (scooter) Happy Rent, Piazza Esquilino 8, ☎ 06 481 8185).
Beach: Spend a day at the beach (➤ 115).
Football: go to a football match (➤ 115).
Concerts and films: go to an outdoor concert or film-screening (➤ 112).
Historic centre: spend half a day wandering around the historic centre, *without a guide book*, or in one of the parks (➤ 58).
Lunch: spend all afternoon having lunch (see list above or ➤ 92–99 for suggestions).
The Pope: listen to the Pope's multi-lingual Wednesday morning address in St Peter's Square (not during the summer).

A civilised lunch is important to Romans

Campo de' Fiori Market; romantic Pincio Hill

Coffee: have a really good coffee ✉ Bar Sant'Eustachio, Piazza Sant'Eustachio 82, ☎ 06 686 1309).

Markets: spend a Sunday morning at Porta Portese flea market, or wander round another of the markets listed (➤ 109).

Window shop, or buy, in the designer area around Via Condotti (➤ 77).

5 Best Ice-Creams

• Giolitti (£) ✉ Via Uffici del Vicario 40 ☎ 06 699 1243. Wide range of flavours.
• Da Mirella (£) ✉ Trastevere end of Ponte Cestio, Isola Tiberina. *Grattachecha* (grated ice served with flavoured syrups or juice) during the summer.
• Il Palazzo del Freddo (£) ✉ Via Principe Eugenio 65–7 ☎ 06 446 4740. Hundreds of different chilled desserts.
• San Calisto ✉ Piazza San Calisto 4. Home-made taste.
• Tre Scalini (£) ✉ Piazza Navona 28–32 ☎ 06 6880 1996. Rich chocolate *tartufi*.

10 Best Churches

• Gesù (➤ 43), for baroque opulence.
• Sant'Andrea al Quirinale (➤ 63), for Bernini.
• San Clemente (➤ 23), for history.
• San Giovanni in Laterano (➤ 65), for history.
• Santa Maria in Domnica (➤ 69), for mosaics.
• Santa Maria Maggiore (➤ 36), for mosaics and history.
• Santa Maria sopra Minerva (➤ 69), for art and originality (a Gothic church, rare for Rome).
• Santa Maria del Popolo (➤ 70), for art.
• Santa Maria in Trastevere (➤ 70) for mosaics.
• St Peter's (➤ 26), for size, importance and everything else.

🕂 29D3
✉ Piazza di Santa Maria
Maggiore
🕐 Daily 7–6:50
Ⓡ Termini, Cavour
🚌 16, 70, 590, 613, 714,
715 to Piazza Santa Maria
Maggiore

Lavish mosaics at
Basilica di San Paolo
Fuori le Mura

BASILICA DI SANTA MARIA MAGGIORE ●●●

On entering you are confronted by the seemingly endless rows of the nave's columns, the sweep of the cosmati floor and a ceiling decorated with the first gold to be brought from the New World. The Sistine (1585) and Pauline (1611) side chapels have opulent works by the most important artists of the day (Maderno, Reni and Ponzio to name but a few). The mosaics are, however, the basilica's glory. On the nave, a 5th-century narrative of the Old Testament and, in the apse, a stunning Glorification of Mary (1295) to whom the church is dedicated, Our Lady herself indicating the site by sending the sign of snowfall in August, an event still celebrated every year. The façade (1743–50) has been restored to its colourful magnificence.

🕂 Off map at 28C1
✉ Via Ostiense 186
🕐 Mon–Sat 7:30–6:45, Sun
7–6:45
Ⓡ San Paolo
🚌 673, 761, 766 to San
Paolo Basilica

🕂 Off map at 29D1
✉ Via Appia Antica
☎ Fri–Wed 9–12, 2:30–5
🚌 118 to San Sebastiano

BASILICA DI SAN PAOLO FUORI LE MURA ●●

Built on the site of St Paul's execution (c67), the present basilica dates from 1874 (Poletti), the original (c386–410) having burnt down in 1823. The only surviving parts are in the transept, the bronze doors (1070), an impressive example of a paschal candlestick (c1190), Arnolfo di Cambio's lovely Gothic *baldacchino* (1285) and the beautiful cloisters (1205–41) with their lavishly decorated mosaic columns (1214, Vassallettis). The general tone, however, is somewhat heavy-handed and 19th-century.

BASILICA DI SAN SEBASTIANO ●

The basilica dates from the first half of the 5th century, on the spot where Peter and Paul's bodies were allegedly buried (their names can be seen in the graffiti on the walls of the catacombs beneath) – the present building dates from the early 17th century. The burial chambers (entered on the left of the façade) also contain exquisite Roman frescoes and stucco work. In pride of place, however, is the crypt of St Sebastian, whose image, pierced by the Diocletian guards' arrows, was particularly popular during the Renaissance. His body lies in the calm white-walled basilica above.

CAMPIDOGLIO (➤ 16, TOP TEN)

CAMPO DE' FIORI ✪✪✪

Since Renaissance times, this has been one of the most bustling, busiest squares in central Rome and is still a great place to drop by at any time of day. Many of the old, crumbling buildings have been restored but the fascinatingly precarious many-layered Palazzo Pio Righetti, set at the square's northeastern corner, still looks as though one of its plant-covered balconies may be about to drop off. During the morning there is a colourful food market which packs up noisily as people saunter to the outdoor restaurants and bars at lunchtime. The foreboding, hooded figure in the centre of the piazza is Giordano Bruno, a philosopher who was burnt at the stake here in 1600 for heresy – the statue was erected when the popes lost their political control of Rome at Italian Unification. The maze of narrow streets that surround the piazza are full of carpenters' and jewellers' workshops, antique and second-hand clothing shops.

🏛 28C3
✉ Piazza Campo de' Fiori
🚌 46, 62, 64 to Corso Vittorio Emanuele

Campo de' Fiori translates as 'field of flowers'; today its market is full of fruit and vegetables

CASTEL SANT'ANGELO (➤ 17, TOP TEN)

CATACOMBS OF SAN CALLISTO ✪

In ancient Rome, when Christianity was still very much a minority religion, it was against the law to bury the dead within the city confines. The catacombs of San Callisto, set in rolling parkland off the Via Appia Antica, are among the largest and most visited. Here there are thought to be a total of 20km of underground galleries on four levels lined with niches, or *loculi*, cut into the rock in which the shrouded bodies of the dead were laid to rest behind stone. Many of the early popes were buried here. The guided tours (offered in a range of languages including English, French and German) cover about 1km.

🏛 29D1
✉ Via Appia Antica 110
☎ 513 6725
🕐 Thu–Tue 8:30–12, 2:30–5:30. Closed Wed, Feb
🚌 218, 660 to San Callisto
♿ Moderate

Off map at 29E5
✉ Via Salaria 430
🕐 Tue–Sun 8:30–12, 2:30–5
🚌 56, 319 to Santa Priscilla
Moderate

CATACOMBS OF SANTA PRISCILLA ⭐⭐

These are probably the most charming of Rome's many catacomb complexes, in the Trieste area, northeast of the centre. The guided tour of the 50m-deep galleries, where 40,000 early Christians were laid to rest, is led by polyglot nuns and includes the earliest-known picture of the Virgin (2nd century AD) and a chapel with frescoes of bible stories. Priscilla was the widow of a Christian who was martyred by Emperor Domitian; the catacombs were dug under the foundations of Priscilla's house.

✚ 28B3
✉ Piazza della Chiesa Nuova
🕐 8–12, 4.30–7
🚌 46, 62, 64 to Piazza della Chiesa Nuova

CHIESA NUOVA ⭐

This was one of the churches which helped to transform the face of Rome in the Catholic resurgence of the 17th century. It is the seat of one of the most important Counter-Reformatory movements, St Phillip Neri's Oratorians. He originally wanted the nave simply white-washed but did not reckon on the exuberant baroque fresco cycles that were to make their dazzling mark in Roman churches half a century later. The breath-taking example here is Pietro di Cortona's (on the nave ceiling, dome and apse, 1647–56). Next door is the brilliant Borromini's superb Oratory façade (1637–40), which is cunningly detailed.

> ### Did you know ?
>
> *Filippo Neri (1515–95), the founder of the Oratorian order for whom Chiesa Nuova was built, was a Florentine banker who had a sudden conversion to Christianity and came to Rome. The emphasis he put on helping the poor, sick, old and young helped him to attract many followers, even though he is said to have made the richer ones humble themselves by dressing in rags.*

The Chiesa Nuova set the style for Roman churches in the 17th century

CIRCO MASSIMO ✪✪✪

There is not much of this ancient racetrack left but you can make out the tight oval that the charioteers careered round and the sloped side on which there was tiered seating for up to 300,000 spectators. The remains of that seating can still be seen at the circus's southern end, although the tower there is medieval. Chariot races were held here from the 4th century BC until they went out of fashion in the 6th century AD. The site was also used for wild-animal fights, mock sea battles (for which it was flooded), athletics and mass executions.

🞤 28C2
✉ Circo Massimo
🚇 Circo Massimo
🚌 60, 75, 81, 160, 175, 628, 673, trams 13, 30B to Circo Massimo
♿ Possible
✋ Free

COLOSSEUM (COLOSSEO) (▶ 18, TOP TEN)

COLUMN OF MARCUS AURELIUS ✪

In the square outside Palazzo Chigi, the prime minister's official residence, and the offices of newspaper *Il Tempo*, is an intricately carved column erected in honour of Emperor Marcus Aurelius after his death in AD 180. It is about 30m high and depicts scenes from the Emperor's successful German campaign. The statue of St Paul at the top of the column replaced the original of Marcus Aurelius on the orders of Pope Sixtus V in 1588.

🞤 28C3
✉ Piazza Colonna
🚌 119 to Piazza Colonna; 56, 60, 62, 81, 85, 95, 160, 175, 492, 628 to Via del Corso

DOMUS AUREA ✪✪

Reopened to the public in 1999, after nearly 20 years of restoration, the Domus Aurea is Emperor Nero's 'Golden House'. After the great fire of AD 64 destroyed over half the city (and when Nero acquired his fiddling reputation), he built this huge symbol of Imperial power over the ruins. It is adorned with elegant fresco cycles and paintings. Tickets must be booked in advance.

🞤 29D3
✉ Via della Domus Aurea, Colle Oppio
☎ 06 6397 49907
🕐 Daily 9–8
🚇 Colosseo
🚌 75, 81, 85, 87, 175 to Colosseo
✋ Moderate

FONTANA DELLE TARTARUGHE ✪✪

This delightfully delicate fountain, in Piazza Mattei, showing four male nymphs with tantalisingly enigmatic smiles cavorting provocatively around its edges, was the work of Giacomo della Porta and Taddeo Landini in the 1580s. The contrastingly precarious tortoises are believed to have been added by Bernini in the following century According to legend the fountain was erected overnight by the Duke of Mattei who wanted to show his potential father-in-law that he was still capable of achieving great things even though he had just lost his fortune. He also had one of the windows of his palace blocked up so that nobody else would ever see it from that superb vantage point.

🞤 28C3
✉ Piazza Mattei
🚌 44, 56, 60, 75, 170, 181, 710, 719 to Via Arenula

The beautiful Fontana delle Tartarughe is a landmark in one of the most elegant squares in central Rome

🕀 28C3
✉ Piazza di Trevi
🚌 56, 58, 60, 61, 62, 95,
115, 119, 175, 492, 590
to Via del Tritone; 81, 85,
160, 628 to Via del Corso

FONTANA DI TREVI

Even without Anita Ekberg, famous for the *Dolce Vita* scene in which she immerses herself in its turbulent waters, this effusively over-the-top fountain is a must for any visitor to Rome (and anyone with any intention of returning to the city should make sure they throw a coin into it). It was designed by Nicolò Salvi in 1762 and shows Neptune flanked by two massive steeds representing the calm and stormy sea bursting out of an artificial cliff-face which contrasts beautifully with the calm orderliness of the Palazzo Poli in whose wall it is built. The panels across the top depict the finding of the spring that feeds the ancient Roman canal leading into the fountain. By the way, the water is now said to contain bleach.

🕀 28C3
✉ Via dei Fori Imperiali
🚇 Colosseo
🚌 85, 87, 175, 186 to Via
dei Fori Imperiali

Above: *remains of smaller
forums exist alongside
the Roman Forum;*
Opposite: *the Fontana di
Trevi is a must for
anyone's agenda*

FORI IMPERIALI

Opposite and next to the main Roman Forum (➤ 22) lie the remaining fragments of five other, smaller, forums each built by an emperor to accommodate the oversp when the original forum became too small to cope with the demands of an expanding empire. To the right of the main entrance to the Roman Forum, underneath the Vittorio Emanuele Monument (➤ 46) is the oldest of these, built by Julius Caesar in AD 51; on the other side of the wide avenue that Mussolini built over other ancient remains to act as a triumphal route up to his Palazzo Venezia headquarters (➤ 56) are the remains of the forums of Trajan (Mercati Traianei ➤ 46), Augustus (where you can see some fine columns and friezes), Vespasian and Nerva.

THE FORUM (FORO ROMANO) (➤ 22, TOP TEN)

GALLERIA BORGHESE ○○○

Finally, after years of restoration work, the whole gallery (both sculpture and painting sections) reopened in summer 1997. The sculpture collection, on the ground floor, includes some important classical works, such as a *Sleeping Hermaphrodite* and a *Dancing Faun*, and the famous Canova sculpture of Paolina Bonaparte Borghese as a reclining Venus. The highlights, however, are the spectacular sculptures by Bernini. Cardinal Scipione Borghese, who had the villa and park built between 1608 and 1615, was Bernini's first patron. Here the sculptor's precocious talent is evident in works such as *The Rape of Proserpine*, *David* (thought to be a self-portrait) and *Daphne and Apollo*. The paintings are on the ground-floor walls and upstairs. Among the celebrated works are a *Deposition* by Raphael, Titian's early masterpiece, *Sacred and Profane Love*, a restored *Last Supper* by Jacopo Bassano, now rich and vibrant, Correggio's erotic *Danae*, and fine works by Guercino, Veronese, Giorgione and Andrea del Sarto. Caravaggio is represented here by six paintings, including one of his most important early works, the luscious *Boy with a Fruit Basket*, the *Sick Bacchus* and also the wonderfully realistic *Madonna of the Serpent*.

Canova's reclining Paolina Bonaparte Borghese

🕀 29D4
✉ Piazzale Scipione Borghese 5, Villa Borghese
☎ 06 854 8577/328101
🕐 Tue–Sat 9–7, Sun, hol 9–1
🍴 Bar
Ⓜ Spagna
🚌 52, 53, 116 to Via Pinciana
♿ Moderate

GALLERIA NAZIONALE D'ARTE MODERNA E CONTEMPORANEA ✪

Cesare Bazzini's *Belle Epoque* palace is one of the few remaining buildings erected for the Rome International Exhibition of 1911 in the northwest area of the park of Villa Borghese. The collection covers the 19th and 20th centuries, mostly Italian artists – De Chirico, the Futurists and the *macchiaioli* (Italy's answer to the French Impressionists) – although there are also works by Gustav Klimt, Paul Cézanne and Henry Moore. Major temporary exhibitions are also staged. The museum has been extensively renovated, long-closed wings are being opened up, there is a new sculpture section, and important contemporary acquisitions have been made.

🕀 28C5
✉ Viale delle Belle Arti 131
☎ 06 322981
🕐 Tue–Sat 9–7, Sun, hol 9–1
🚋 Trams 19, 30B to Viale delle Belle Arti
♿ Moderate
↔ Villa Giulia (➤ 78)

IL GESÙ ⭐⭐

This church spans the whole of the baroque: from the floor plan (by Vignola, 1568, and probably based on the ideas of one of Michelangelo's last architectural plans), through the façade (with its triangular pediment and side scrolls) and dome (by Giacomo della Porta, 1575) to Pietro da Cortona's altar of St Xavier (1674) and Andrea Pozzo's almost vulgarly ornate chapel of St Ignatius (1696). This is the central church of the Jesuits, the severe order founded by Ignatius Loyola in the 16th century – its design has been imitated in Jesuit church-building all over the world. Next door are the rooms occupied by Loyola (usually open when the church is) which have a wonderful *trompe l'oeil* fresco by Pozzo.

28C3
Piazza del Gesù
Oct–Mar, 6–12:30, 4:30–7:15; Apr–Sep, 6–12:30, 4–7:30
44, 46, 60, 62, 64, 70, 81, 87, 115, 186, 492, 710 to Largo di Torre Argentina

THE GHETTO ⭐⭐

The Jewish community in Rome is one of the oldest in Europe and dates from the 1st century BC, although it first settled this area north of Isola Tiberina (► 45) in the 13th century. From the mid-16th century until Italian Unification in 1870 Roman Jews were enclosed behind high walls in this warren of narrow, winding alleyways which still house kosher butchers, excellent Jewish restaurants and a baker offering Roman Jewish specialities such as *torta di ricotta* and sweet 'pizzas' made with candied and dried fruit. At the heart of the ghetto was the old fish market held in front of the Portico d'Ottavia, the only remains of a vast shop and temple complex, which was renovated in the 1st century BC and named in honour of Emperor Augustus's sister Octavia.

28C3
Via del Portico d'Ottavia (and the streets north)
44, 46, 60, 62, 64, 70, 81, 87, 115, 492 to Largo di Torre Argentina; 8 to Via Arenula

Below: *Gianicolo hill takes its name from the god Janus*

GIANICOLO ⭐⭐

The hill that rises between Trastevere and the Vatican to the southwest of the Tiber has some of the best views of central Rome and is a popular lovers' tryst. At its summit is Piazza Giuseppe Garibaldi, where a rousing equestrian statue of Giuseppe Garibaldi commemorates his 1849 victory over the French here when he led the troops of the Roman Republic in the struggle for Italian unification.

28B3
Viale Aldo Fabrizi
870 to Passeggiata del Gianicolo

Gianicolo to the Ghetto

Distance
4km

Time
2 hours, or 4 with stops for coffee and visits

Start point
Piazza Garibaldi
🔲 28B3
🚌 41

End point
The Ghetto
🔲 28C3
🚌 44

Lunch
Sora Margherita (£)
✉ Piazza delle Cinque Scole 30
☎ 686 4002

The church of San Bartolomeo stands on the tiny Isola Tiberina

Start at Piazza Garibaldi on the Gianicolo (➤ 43).

Follow the road southeast, past the busts of heroes of the Risorgimento, to the gateway, turn left down the staircase.

But first look at the monumental baroque Fontana Paola, where people once washed their clothes.

Follow the road down past the Spanish Embassy and turn left on Via Garibaldi. Go to the bottom where, to the left, is Porta Settimiana (1498), the gateway pilgrims used to reach the Vatican. Turn right down Via della Scala.

The church of Santa Maria della Scala dates from the late 16th century. Its plain façade hides a rich, cluttered interior.

Continue straight into Piazza San Egidio, past the Museo del Folklore (➤ 48), and turn left, passing Vicolo del Piede and the Pasquino cinema, into Piazza Santa Maria in Trastevere.

Here are the church (➤ 70), with its 12th-century mosaics on the façade, and fountain by Carlo Fontana (1692).

Continue straight through the piazza and follow Via della Lungaretta to Piazza Sonnino.

On the right is the 12th-century bell tower of the ancient church of San Crisogono, rebuilt in the 16th century.

Cross the piazza. The left-corner tower is 13th-century and home to the Dante Society. Go on to Piazza di Piscinula, turn left up a staircase along the side of an old palace and cross the Lungotevere to get to Isola Tiberina (➤ 45).

Isola Tiberina somewhat resembles a ship and was a strategic point in ancient times being one of the few points at which the Tiber could be easily crossed.

Cross the island to the Ghetto (➤ 43); on the right is the Synagogue (1874) and a small museum. This area is a good lunch stop.

ISOLA TIBERINA

From the right-hand (Ghetto-) side of the river, Isola Tiberina is reached via the oldest original bridge over the Tiber, the Ponte Fabricio (62 BC). Originally the walls of the buildings rose directly out of the river but, since the end of the 19th century, the island has been surrounded by a wide embankment, now a popular spot for taking early-season sun. The church of San Bartolomeo was built in the 10th century on the site of a 3rd-century BC temple to the god of healing, Aesculapius, and the connection with health has been continued by the Fatebenefratelli hospital which now covers most of the island. Downstream you can see the one remaining arch of the Ponte Rotto (broken bridge) which was the first stone bridge in Rome (142 BC), although it had already fallen down at least twice before this mid-16th-century rebuild collapsed in 1598.

:heavy_plus_sign: 28C2
:envelope: Isola Tiberina
:bus: 717, 774, 780 to Lungotevere dei Cenci or to Lungotevere Anguillara

KEATS-SHELLEY MEMORIAL HOUSE

Since 1909 the house at the foot of the Spanish Steps, where Keats died of consumption aged only 25 in February 1821, has been a memorial to Keats, Shelley, Byron and other romantic poets. The rooms which Keats occupied on the first floor now contain a collection of manuscripts, documents and ephemera including Keats's death mask and a lock of his hair. There is also an extensive specialist library. There is a **Landmark Trust** flat on the 3rd floor.

The Landmark Trust
This charity rescues buildings, and lets them out for holidays. When the Keats-Shelley Memorial Association launched an appeal for funds to maintain the Keats-Shelley Memorial House, the Trust took on the 3rd-floor flat, restoring it to its appearance in about 1800. The sitting room overlooks the Spanish Steps. Handbook and prices from: The Landmark Trust, Shottesbrooke, Maidenhead, Berkshire SL6 3SW, UK (☎ 01628 825925).

:heavy_plus_sign: 28C4
:envelope: Piazza di Spagna 26
:telephone: 06 678 4235
:clock: Summer, Mon–Fri 9–1, 3–6; winter, Mon–Fri 9–1, 2:30–5.30
:metro: Spagna
:bus: 119 to Piazza di Spagna
:hand: Moderate

LARGO ARGENTINA

Behind one of the busiest bus intersections in the Area Sacra at Largo Argentina are the remains of four Republican-era temples, known as temples A, B, C and D (in alphabetical order starting nearest the main bus stop). Temple C is the oldest (4th century BC) while 3rd-century BC Temple A was used as a church during the Middle Ages (remains of two apses); behind it are the drains of a massive public toilet. Julius Caesar was murdered near here in 44BC when the Senate were using the Curia of Pompey as a temporary meeting place while the main senate house was being restored. The area is rarely open to the public.

:heavy_plus_sign: 28C3
:envelope: Largo di Torre Argentina
:clock: Some evenings in summer for guided tours in English and Italian
:bus: 44, 46, 56, 60, 62, 65, 70, 81, 87, 94, 115, 186, 492, to Largo di Torre Argentina

Right: This statue stands before the Vittorio Emanuele Monument, built to celebrate the first King of Unified Italy

---

Did you know ?

Until the end of the 19th century, Piazza Venezia was the finishing point of the riderless horse races that were held at Carnevale (the week before Lent begins) down Via del Corso from Piazza del Popolo. The horses were urged on by the use of stimulants, fireworks and ropes studded with nails that were tied around their bodies. The Museo del Folklore (➤ 48) has some contemporary engravings of the event.

🕂 28C3
✉ Clivo Argentario 1, Via di San Pietro in Carcere
☎ 06 679 2902
🕐 Oct–Mar, 9–12, 2:30–5; Apr–Sep, 9–12, 2:30–6
🚌 44, 46, 81, 95, 160, 170, 181, 628, 713, 719 to Piazza Venezia
💷 Donation

MAMERTINE PRISON (CARCERE MAMERTINO)   ✪

This dank, dark dungeon dates from the 4th century BC and was where any potential threats to state security, including the leaders of opposing armies, were thrown to starve to death (their bodies were dropped into the main sewer, the Cloaca Maxima). St Peter is said to have been imprisoned here before being crucified and an altar has been built next to the spring that he miraculously created in order to christen other prisoners and two of his guards.

🕂 28C3
✉ Via IV Novembre 94
☎ 06 679 0048
🕐 Tue–Sun 9–7
🚌 60, 64, 70, 170 to Via IV Novembre
♿ Limited
💷 Cheap; free last Sun of month

MERCATI TRAIANEI   ✪✪

One of the first shopping malls in the world, Emperor Trajan commissioned this five-level complex of about 150 small shops from the Greek architect Apollodorus of Damascus in the early 2nd century AD. Goods from all over the empire were sold here and shops were probably arranged by area – storage jars found on the first floor suggest that wine and oil were sold here while fruit and flower shops probably occupied the ground floor. The finely carved column next to the markets was erected in AD 113 to celebrate Trajan's campaigns in Dacia (Romania). It is 40m high and originally bore a statue of the emperor which was replaced by the present St Peter in 1587.

🕂 28C3
✉ Piazza Venezia
🚌 44, 46, 81, 95, 160, 170, 175, 181, 628, 710, 713, 719 to Piazza Venezia

MONUMENTO A VITTORIO EMANUELE II   ✪✪

A monument of many names; il Vittoriale was built at the end of the 19th century to honour the first king of the united Italy whose equestrian statue stands out proudly in front. Behind him burns the eternal flame guarded day and night by armed soldiers at the Altar of the Nation while other, less complimentary, ways of referring to this colon-naded mass of white marble include the 'typewriter' and the 'wedding cake'. In any event, you cannot miss it.

🕂 Off map south
✉ Viale Lincoln 3, EUR
☎ 592 6148

MUSEO DELL'ALTO MEDIOEVO   ✪

This museum houses decorative arts of the 5th to 11th centuries (from the fall of the Roman Empire to the Renaissance). Most of the artefacts were found locally, and include some beautiful jewellery from the 7th century, fragments of elaborate embroidery from clerical robes and a delicate 5th-century gold fibula found on the Palatine hill. Swords made from gold and silver, intricately carved and decorated, demonstrate how objects made from pure metals can withstand the test of time better than more reactive ones.

MUSEO DELLE ARTI E TRADIZIONI POPOLARI ✪

A huge collection of fascinating objects relating to Italian folk art and rural traditions. On display are agricultural and pastoral tools, including elaborately decorated carts and horse tack, artisan instruments and handiwork, clothing, furniture, musical instruments, some exquisite traditional jewellery and photographs documenting how the exhibits were used.

🕐 Mon–Sat 9–2, Sun, hol 9–1:30
Ⓜ Magliana
🚌 714, 715 to Piazzale G Marconi
👆 Cheap

✚ Off map south
✉ Piazza G Marconi 8, EUR
☎ 06 592 6148
🕐 Mon–Sat 9–2, Sun 9–1
Ⓜ Magliana
🚌 714, 715
👆 Cheap

28B3
Corso Vittorio Emanuele II 158
06 6880 6848
Tue–Sat 9–7, Sun, hol 9–1
46, 62, 64 to Corso Vittorio Emanuele
None
Cheap

MUSEO BARRACCO ★

This is one of Rome's most charming museums but often overlooked. The exquisite, small collection of Assyrian, Egyptian, Greek and Roman sculptures (including a series of Roman heads minus their noses) and artefacts was created by Senator Giovanni Barracco and presented to the city in 1902. Underneath the museum (ask the attendants to take you down) are remains of what is said to be a Roman fish shop, complete with counter and a water trough. Fresco fragments (from the 4th century AD) found there are displayed on the ground floor.

Off map at 28C1
Piazza Gianni Agnelli 10, EUR
06 592 6041
Tue–Sat 9–7, Sun, hol 9–1
Magliana
714, 715 to Piazza G. Marconi
Moderate
Museo dell'Alto Medioevo, Museo Nazionale delle Arti e Tradizioni Popolari

Models recreate in detail early Roman life for us

MUSEO DELLA CIVILTÀ ROMANA ★

The models and reconstructions inside this grandly fascist building give a sense of what life was really like in ancient

Rome and help put into context the fragments and artefacts that are the treasures of so many of the city's museums. There are busts and statues of the key figures of the day, reproductions of Roman furniture, surgical tools, musical instruments and sundials. The highlight is a giant scale model of Rome in the 4th century AD, at the time of Constantine, showing every building within the circular Aurelian walls.

28B2
Piazza Sant'Egidio 1/b
06 581 6563
Tue–Sat 9–7, Sun 9–1
280 to Lungotevere Sanzio; 64, 70, 71, 87, 492 to Largo Argentina then tram 8 to Viale di Trastevere
Cheap

MUSEO DEL FOLKLORE E DEI POETI ROMANESCHI ★

The museum opened in 1978 in a former Carmelite convent behind the church of Santa Maria in Trastevere. Everyday life in 17th- and 18th-century Italy, including festivals and customs, is illustrated by paintings, prints, reconstructions and waxworks, all among an interesting diversity of artefacts from the period when the popes ruled Rome. There is also memorabilia relating to famous Roman poets including Giuseppe Gioacchino Belli and Carlo Alberto Salustri (better known as Trilussa). Each of these local-dialect poets appropriately has a Trastevere square named after him.

28B3
Via Zanardelli 1
06 6880 6286
Tue–Sat 9–7, Sun, hols 9–1
70, 81, 87, 115, 119, 186, 492, 628 to Via Zanardelli
Cheap

MUSEO NAPOLEONICO ★

This collection of art and memorabilia relating to Napoleon includes portraits by David and Gerard, political cartoons, uniforms and the audacious French general's baby teeth. Napoleon was only in Rome for a short time, although his mother and sister Paolina, who married Prince Camillo Borghese, settled here. Paolina was portrayed by Canova as Venus (▶ 42) and a cast of her breast is on display.

MUSEO NAZIONALE DELLE PASTE ALIMENTARI ✪

A visit to this well-organised museum will tell you everything you ever needed to know about pasta (and a lot more besides). A portable CD player provides commentary (in Italian, English, Japanese, French or German) to the displays. The entire gamut of pasta production is covered, and there are examples of equipment and machinery used over the years, some rather questionable artworks on the pasta theme and photos of Italian and international personalities tucking into steaming plates of the nation's favourite dish.

76B1
Piazza Scanderberg 117
06 699 1119
Mon–Sun 9:30–5:30
81, 85, 160, 628 to Via del Corso
Expensive

MUSEO NAZIONALE ROMANO ✪✪

The beautifully restored Palazzo Massimo is a fine example of how Rome pulled out all the stops for the Holy Year (2000) and gave the national collection of ancient art and sculpture a setting it deserves. The upper floors are bursting with more archaeological goodies from the Roman age (2nd century BC to 4th century AD) such as some exquisite mosaics from Livia's palace and a superb marble statue of a discus thrower (a Roman copy of a 5th-century BC Greek bronze). It's definitely worth equipping yourself with a well-illustrated guidebook from the museum's excellent shop to negotiate your route around the extensive displays.

Spacious and airy rooms open onto a central courtyard, the exhibits are clearly labelled and each room has information sheets in English and Italian. You are greeted by a huge alabaster and basalt statue of Minerva, then follow several rooms of portrait busts from the 3rd to 1st centuries BC, painted friezes, mosaics, sarcophagi and intricately carved pedestals. An extensive collection of coins dating back to the 7th century BC is one of the highlights.

29D4
67 Piazza dei Cinquecento
06 4890 3500
Tue–Sat 9–7, Sun, hol 9–2
Termini
36, 38, 40, 60, 64, 65, 105, 115, 170, 175, 310, 317, 319, 613, 714, 715, 910 to Termini
Good
Moderate

Wander past every type of ancient Roman sculpture in the Museo Nazionale Romano's vast cloister

Food & Drink

Italian cuisine is among the best (and, according to research, the most healthy) in the world. Each region has its own particular specialities, making use of the abundant raw ingredients that grow there, and some typically Roman dishes also owe much to the history of the city and its occupants.

Pasta

Classic Roman pasta dishes are *spaghetti alla carbonara* with bacon, eggs and *pecorino* (matured sheep's milk cheese, often used as an alternative to parmesan); *pasta all'arrabbiata* ('angry pasta' means hot) with tomatoes and fiery hot *peperoncino* (chilli); and *all'Amatriciana*, which is more or less the same with added bacon. *Pasta e ceci* is like a thick soup made with small pasta and chick peas, while *gnocchi* are hunger-busting potato dumplings served with butter and sage or tomato sauce.

Above: *speciality pasta in many shapes and colours*

Below: *making pizza*

Meat and Offal

Tradition has it that, while most of the butchered animal went to the rich, poor Romans had to make do with the left-over offal. This has led to an abundance of dishes using tripe, liver, kidneys, heart, bone marrow (*ossobuco* is a bone out of which the marrow is scooped) and brains. Perhaps the most extreme of these is *pagliata*, which is the intestine of a milk-fed calf, often served with *bucatini*, the thin, tube-like pasta it resembles. The best place for eating offal is in Testaccio where restaurants around the ex-abattoir Mattatoio have a long tradition of this type of cuisine.

Nowadays, however, even the most basic *trattoria* will offer beef and veal steaks, sausages (often with brown lentils) and flavoursome lamb from nearby Abruzzo. *Saltimbocca alla Romana* ('jumps into the mouth') is veal wrapped in raw ham and cooked with sage.

Fish

Apart from the traditional *baccalà* (cod fillets fried in batter and served as a snack or first course in *pizzerie*), the range of fish in Rome is immense and includes seafood such as mussels, clams (especially in *spaghetti alle vongole*), squid and prawns.

Vegetables and Snack Foods

Some of the vegetables common in Rome make good snacks – courgette flowers fried in batter, artichokes either steamed or baked, potato or spinach croquettes. *Supplì*, rice croquettes with a melted mozzarella filling, are another between-meals filler.

Other vegetables include *fave* (broad beans), often eaten with *pecorino* cheese in spring, spinach, broccoli, rocket and *puntarelle*, a crispy salad vegetable served in a vinegary sauce with anchovies.

Wines and Drinks

In Rome most of the house white wines come from Frascati and the Castelli Romani that surround the city. Orvieto in Umbria is another source of inexpensive white wine. House reds come from slightly further afield, Montepulciano from Abruzzo (not to be confused with the Vino Nobile of Montepulciano in Tuscany, which is a top-quality wine) and Chianti from Tuscany.

As well as wine, Italy has a massive range of drinks to stimulate the appetite before you eat or to help you digest the meal afterwards. *Aperitivi* include Campari and Martini-type aromatics, *prosecco*, a light fizzy white wine and *analcolici*, non-alcoholic versions of Campari and Martini. *Digestivi* include grappas that range from firewater to the smoothest of the smooth and *amari*, those thick, sticky concoctions made with herbs.

Fresh fish on sale at Campo de' Fiori

Dolci

If you don't opt for the ubiquitous *tiramisu*, for which nearly every restaurant has its own subtly different recipe, you could finish your meal with a slice of cake (*torta*); chocolate, fruit or *torta della nonna* with custard and pine kernels. Especially in winter, you'll be offered *crème caramel*, *crème brulée*, *panna cotta* ('cooked cream', a thick but light custard often served with berries), or ice-cream.

Frascati and Orvieto, two local sources for house white wines

PALATINO ●●●

Attached to the Forum (admission includes both), this is a peaceful, lush, hilly area covered with the remains of the massive palaces that the Roman emperors built for themselves. Most of what is on view dates from the 1st century AD. It can be frustrating to visit because many of the main attractions close at short notice and little is labelled, but there are guaranteed views of the Forum

(► 22) from the delightful semi-formal Orti Farnesiani (Farnese Gardens), laid out for Cardinal Alessandro Farnese in the 16th century. Underneath the gardens is a long tunnel built by Nero and decorated with stucco reliefs, some of which have survived. He may have intended this as a promenade for hot weather although some researchers believe that it led all the way to his massive palace overlooking the spot where the Colosseum stands today. Other highlights of the Palatine (although not always accessible) include the baths of Septimus Severus, the wall paintings in the house of Livia, traces of an 8th century BC village of huts and the complicated ground floor layouts of the Domus Flavia and the Domus Augustana.

Ruins of Roman palaces cover the Palatine Hill

Through the Forum or Via di San Gregorio
06 699 0110
(► 22) for hours
Colosseo, Circo Massimo
75, 81, 175, 673 to Via di San Gregorio
28C2

PALAZZO BARBERINI (► 19, TOP TEN)

PALAZZO COLONNA ●●

Some of the most beautiful ceiling frescoes in Rome adorn the opulent 18th-century galleries. There are some fine portraits in the first room but the eye automatically wanders through to the lavishly gilded Great Hall with its magnificent ceiling painting representing the life of Marcantonio Colonna. As you step down take care not to trip over the cannonball which became lodged there during the siege of Rome in 1849. Two ornate cabinets – one with inlaid carved ivory panels reproducing works by Raphael and Michelangelo (the central panel is his *Last Judgement* from the Sistine Chapel) – give the Room of the Desks its name. The Apotheosis of the Colonna Pope Martin V decorates the ceiling of the fourth room where Annibale Caracci's delightful *Bean Eater* makes an amusing change from more serious subjects. In the Throne Room a chair is kept ready (turned to the wall) in case of a papal visit.

28C3
Via della Pilotta 17
06 679 4362
Sat 9–1
40, 44, 46, 60, 81, 94, 95, 160, 170, 181, 628, 710, 713, 719 to Piazza Venezia
Expensive

PALAZZO CORSINI ✪✪

Once the residence of Queen Christina of Sweden (► 14), the palace houses part of the national art collection (the more important part is at Palazzo Barberini, (► 19). The galleries, decorated with arresting *trompe l'oeil* frescoes, are filled predominantly with paintings from the 16th and 17th centuries. In room 1 Van Dyck's superb *Madonna della Paglia* and Murillo's *Madonna and Child* stand out among many other paintings of the same subject; one by Girolamo Siciolante de Sermoneta is frightening in its awfulness with an over-rosy, muscular baby seeming to choke on its mother's milk. Do not miss the paintings of the Bologna school in room 7, among which Guido Reni's richly coloured and expressive *St Jerome* and melancholy *Salome*, Giovanni Lanfranco's very beautiful *St Peter Healing St Agatha* and the haunting *Ecce Homo* by Guercino are highlights.

🚹 28B3
✉ Via della Lungara 10
☎ 06 6880 2323
🕐 Tue–Fri 9–7, Sat 9–2, Sun 9–1. Closed Mon
🚌 323, 280 to Lungotevere della Farnesina
♿ Few
💰 Expensive
↔ Villa Farnesina

Looking towards the Palatino from the Forum

PALAZZO DORIA PAMPHILI

The seat of the noble Roman family since the late Renaissance, Palazzo Doria Pamphili takes up an entire block of Via del Corso. Extensive renovations took place in 1996. In the grand reception rooms, through which you enter, and the original picture galleries with their elaborate frescoed ceilings, the paintings are hung exactly as they were in the 18th century, cluttered side by side from floor to ceiling. Four rooms now house masterpieces from the 15th to 17th centuries including works by Hans Memling, Raphael, Titian, Tintoretto and two early paintings by Caravaggio. The star of the collection is the Velasquez portrait of Doria Pope, Innocent X, resplendent in vermilion robes, majestically positioned in its own chamber. For an extra charge take a guided tour of the fascinating private apartments.

PALAZZO DELLE ESPOSIZIONI

Rome's purpose-built (1883) palace of the fine arts has had a chequered history. Apart from serving its original brief, the building has housed the Communist Party, been a mess for allied servicemen, a polling station and a public lavatory. After years of restoration it was relaunched in 1990, and is today a vibrant multi-media centre with a strong emphasis on film and video in addition to an active programme of Italian and international exhibitions (both historical and contemporary). Good museum marketing has taken over and there is an excellent shop, a pleasant indoor café and a roof garden.

PALAZZO MADAMA

This pretty little palace has been the seat of the Italian senate since 1871, hence the armed police and military guard. It was built as the Medici family's Roman residence in the 16th century although the Madame after whom it was named was Margaret of Parma, an illegitimate daughter of Emperor Charles V who lived here in the 1560s. The icing-like stucco façade of cherubs and fruit was added in the 17th century.

PALAZZO DI MONTECITORIO

Bernini did the original designs for this concave palace, although all that remains of his work are the clock-tower, the columns and the window sills. In 1871 it became the Chamber of Deputies and had doubled in size by 1918. In the sloping piazza in front of the palace there are often political demonstrations; a strong police presence keeps people at a respectful distance from the main entrance

through which Italy's 630 parliamentarians enter and exit. The obelisk in the piazza was brought from Egypt by Augustus in 10 BC to act as the pointer of a giant (but, due to subsidence, inaccurate) sundial in nearby Campo Marzio. It was re-erected here in 1787.

Palazzo Doria Pamphili is dazzling even by Roman standards

PALAZZO DEL QUIRINALE ✪✪

This large orange palace, with the picture-book round look-out tower to its left, is the official residence of the President of the Republic of Italy and is guarded by exotically uniformed *Granatieri* who have been specially selected for their height and good looks. It was built in the 1570s as a papal summer palace for the fresh air on the highest of Rome's seven hills. Opposite, the two massive men with somewhat under-sized horses are ancient Roman copies of a 5th-century BC Greek sculpture of Castor and Pollux, the two god-knights who came to Rome's rescue during an early battle. The palace is open to the public on the second and fourth Sunday of the month from September through to July.

✚ 28C3
✉ Piazza del Quirinale
🚌 64, 70, 75, to Via IV Novembre

Italian Navy band marching out of the Quirinale

Discover Borromini's clever trompe l'oeil perspective in the courtyard of Palazzo Spada

✚ 28B3
✉ Piazza Capo di Ferro 3
☎ 06 686 1158
🕐 Tue–Sat 9–7, Sun, hol 9–1
🚌 280 to Lungotevere dei Tebaldi; 170 to Via Arenula; 40, 64, 70, 71, 492 to Largo Argentina then tram 8
♿ Moderate

PALAZZO SPADA ✪✪

Built in 1540, the ornate palace was acquired by Cardinal Bernardino Spada in the 17th century. In addition to housing his collection in the Galleria Spada, the palace is the seat of the Italian Council of State and thus under prominent *Carabinieri* guard. Among the 17th- and 18th-century paintings are a jewel-like *Visitation* attributed to Andrea del Sarto and works by Guercino and Rubens. Cardinal Spada also collected Roman sculpture – the restored *Seated Philosopher* is a highlight.

The most delightful aspect of the palace is Borromini's ingenious *trompe l'oeil* perspective in the lower courtyard (ask the attendants or porter to let you in). A long colonnade stretches out to a large statue at the end. Go closer to see that the colonnade is in fact only a quarter of the length it seems, and the statue much smaller than it first appears.

✚ 28C3
✉ Via del Plebiscito 118
☎ 06 6999 4243
🕐 Tue–Sun 9–2
🚌 44, 46, 57, 75, 81, 94, 95, 160, 170, 181, 6228, 710, 713, 719 to Piazza Venezia
♿ Few 🛈 Moderate

PALAZZO VENEZIA ✪✪

Rome's most important collection of medieval decorative arts includes fine examples of Byzantine jewellery, silver work, ceramics, porcelain, tapestries and armour. There is a superb group of intricately carved Florentine wooden marriage chests, some small 16th-century bronzes and fine religious paintings by early Renaissance artists. Palazzo Venezia often hosts special exhibitions in the opulent main halls overlooking the piazza. Mussolini used the impressive, vast Sala del Mappamondo as his office.

PANTHEON (► 20, TOP TEN)

PASQUINO

Physically, Pasquino has seen better days; all that remain of this 3rd-century BC sculpture near Piazza Navona, are a twisted torso and a weather-beaten face. But, for several centuries after he was propped up here in the early 16th century Pasquino played an important role as Rome's most talkative 'talking statue'. During the days of papal rule (until 1870) there were few safe outlets for dissent and those with political or social axes to grind came at dead of night to attach their written complaints to one of the talking statues.

28B3
Piazza di Pasquino
46, 622, 64 to Corso Vittorio Emanuele

PIAZZA BARBERINI

The traffic-filled square at the foot of Via Veneto, the street that was the hub of the *Dolce Vita* days of swinging Rome in the 1960s, contains two fountains designed by Bernini in the 1640s for the Barberini family. At the join with Via

28C4
Piazza Barberini
Barberini
60, 61, 62, 492, 590 to Piazza Barberini

Bernini's Fontana della Api in Piazza Barberini

Veneto is the Fontana delle Api whose grotesquely large bees (the Barberini family crest) crawl over the unassuming basin. In the centre of the square is the far more dramatic *Tritone*, whose well-muscled body is supported by his own fish-tail legs and four dolphins as he enthusiastically blows water through a vast sea-shell.

PIAZZA DEI CAVALIERI DI MALTA

Piranesi, famous for his surreal etchings of Roman views, designed this peaceful piazza in 1765 and decorated it with the symbols and devices of the Order of the Knights of Malta whose priory is here. In the door of the priory is a peep-hole which offers a magnificent miniature view of the dome of St Peter's seen beyond the tree-lined avenue of the priory's garden. This part of the city, the Aventine, has always been a genteel residential area.

28C2
Piazza dei Cavalieri di Malta
95, 713, 716 to Lungotevere Aventino

The Historic Centre

Distance
4km

Time
2 hours without stops, 3½ hours with

Start point
Piazza Farnese
 28B3
to Corso Vittorio Emanuele

End point
Piazza del Popolo
28C4
Flaminio
to Piazzale Flaminio

Lunch
Hostaria Romanesca (£)
Campo de' Fiori 40
06 686 4024

Combine this walk with visits to the Forum and the Vatican and you can claim to have 'done' Rome.

From Piazza Farnese take Vicolo dei Baulari into Campo de' Fiori (➤ 37), where you can have an early lunch. Go to the far left-hand corner and into Piazza della Cancelleria.

Palazzo della Cancelleria (now Vatican offices) was built in 1485–1513 for a great-nephew of the Pope.

Turn right on Corso Vittorio Emanuele; cross at the lights. Continue down Via Cuccagna into Piazza Navona. Halfway up the piazza, Corso Agone leads to Palazzo Madama; Via Salvatore runs alongside, to San Luigi dei Francesi on the left. Continue to the Pantheon.

Pause, watch the activity, or have an expensive coffee.

Take the right-hand alley opposite the Pantheon, Vicolo della Maddalena, turn right down Via del Vicario into Piazza del Montecitorio. Follow Via di Guglia, in front of the palazzo, turn left at Via dei Pastini into Piazza di Pietra.

Here there are columns of a 2nd-century AD temple of Hadrian.

Walk past the columns, down Via di Pietra, cross Via del Corso and continue straight up Via di Muratte to the Trevi fountain. Follow Via della Stamperia, right of the fountain, turn right up Via del Tritone, cross and turn left on Via Due Macelli to Piazza di Spagna.

Rest by Bernini's Fontana della Barcaccis to observe the vitality as tourists and shoppers converge.

Climb the Spanish Steps, turn left, past Villa Medici (16th century, now the French Academy), take the path on the right to the Pincio Gardens.

Here are wonderful views over Piazza del Popolo.

PIAZZA FARNESE ⭑⭑

Dominated by Palazzo Farnese, which was designed for Farnese Pope Paulo III in the 1530s by – among others – Michelangelo, this spacious, nearly traffic-free square is a peaceful contrast to the nearby buzz of Campo de' Fiori (➤ 37) and a good spot for a quiet rest. The palace is now the French Embassy and at night Caracci's ceiling paintings on the first floor are illuminated. The two vast granite fountains were assembled in the 17th century from bath-tubs found at Caracalla's baths (➤ 75). They are decorated with lilies, the Farnese family crest.

🔲 28B3
✉ Piazza Farnese
🚌 46, 62, 64 to Corso Vittorio Emanuele

PIAZZA NAVONA (➤ 21, TOP TEN)

PIAZZA DEL POPOLO ⭑⭑⭑

For the Grand Tourists of the 18th and 19th centuries this was the first sight of Rome as their luggage-laden carriages trundled through the Porta del Popolo. It was also where condemned criminals were executed (by having their heads smashed with hammers until the more humane guillotine took over in the early 19th century). It is overlooked to the east by the Pincio Gardens, which has marvellous views over the historic city centre and to the Vatican. The two apparently identical churches at the end of Via del Corso were built in the late 17th century by Rainaldi; looks can deceive though and, to fit into the available space, one of them actually has an oval rather than a round dome.

🔲 28C4
✉ Piazza del Popolo
Ⓜ Flaminio

🚌 119, 590 to Piazza del Popolo; 95, 125, 490, 495, 926, and tram 225 Piazzale Flaminio

Domenico Fontana designed the fountain (1589) around the 3,000-year-old obelisk that Emperor Augustus brought from Egypt.

Looking down the Via del Corso from Piazza del Popolo

PIAZZA DELLA REPUBBLICA ⭑

A rather seedy square whose once elegant colonnade is now occupied by adult cinemas and tourist-trapping bars, one side is dominated by the 3rd-century AD remains of the baths of Diocletian, into which Michelangelo incorporated the church of Santa Maria degli Angeli in 1563. The enticingly voluptuous nymphs (1901) of Mario Rutelli's *Fontana delle Naiadi* were greeted with scandalised horror when they were unveiled in 1910, but they have aged badly and their bodies are pock-marked by pollution.

🔲 29D3
✉ Piazza della Repubblica
Ⓜ Repubblica
🚌 40, 60, 64, 70, 115, 116, 170 to Piazza della Repubblica

✚ 28C4
✉ Piazza di Spagna
Ⓢ Spagna
🚌 119 to Piazza di Spagna

The perennially popular Spanish Steps afford a bird's-eye view across the city

PIAZZA DI SPAGNA

The sweeping Spanish Steps, designed in 1720 to connec the piazza with the French church of Trinità dei Monti, are now usually smothered with tourists, Italian soldiers and street-vendors who compete for space with tubs of magnolias in springtime and a life-size nativity scene at Christmas. The piazza gets its name from the Spanish Embassy which was here in the 17th century, and has been a compulsory stop for visitors to Rome since the 18th and 19th centuries when local tradesmen, models, unemployed servants and beggars mingled hopefully with the foreign artists, writers and Grand Tourists who congregated here Keats lived and died in an apartment here (▶ 45). The low-

lying Fontana della Barcaccia (fountain of the broken boat) at the bottom of the steps was designed by Pietro Bernini, father of the more famous Gian Lorenzo, in 1627 for Barberini Pope Urban VIII; the bees and suns were taken from the Barberini family crest. To the southeast, in Piazza Mignanelli, is a statue of the Virgin Mary on top of a column. This was erected in 1857 when Pope Pius IX proclaimed the doctrine of the Immaculate Conception, holding that the Virgin was the only person ever to have been born without original sin.

Attractive Ponte Sant'Angelo incorporates arches of Emperor Hadrian's original bridge, the Pons Aelius

PIRAMIDE CESTIA ✪

An engineer could tell you that this is nothing like as well-built as the Egyptian originals that inspired magistrate Caius Cestis (in Italian, *Caio Cestio*) when he was designing his own tomb in the 1st century BC – a time when the fashion for all things Egyptian was at its height. For all that, this 27m-high pyramid has stood the test of time and makes a somewhat surreal landmark next to the Porta San Paolo, one of the original gateways into Rome.

✚ 28C1
✉ Piazzale Ostiense
Ⓜ Piramide
🚌 57, 75, 175, 673, 716 and trams 13, 30B to Piramide
↔ Protestant Cemetery

PONTE SANT'ANGELO ✪✪

Certainly the most elegant of the bridges over the Tiber, Bernini designed the ten angels which adorn its balustrades, each displaying one of the devices of Christ's passion, in 1667. Their ecstatically swooning expressions earned them the nickname of the 'Breezy Maniacs'. (Two more angels, deemed too beautiful to withstand the rigours of the Roman climate, are on show in the church of Sant'Andrea delle Fratte in Via di Sant'Andrea delle Fratte.) Most of the bridge dates from the 17th and 19th centuries but the central arches are the remains of the bridge that Emperor Hadrian built here in the 1st century AD to lead to his tomb (now Castel Sant'Angelo, ► 17).

✚ 28B3
✉ Ponte Sant'Angelo
Ⓜ Lepanto
🚌 87, 280, 492 to Lungotevere Castello; 49, 70, 926, 990 to Piazza Cavour

Via Appia Antica (The Appian Way)

Distance
9km (3km to tomb of Cecilia Metella)

Time
Whole walk with minimum of stops 3 hours; to tomb of Cecilia Metella 1 hour without stops, 2–3 hours with stops

Start point
Porta di San Sebastiano
➕ 29D1
🚌 118

End point
Via Appia Nuova
➕ 29E1
🚌 663, 664

Lunch
Cecilia Metella (➤ 93); beyond this there are no bars or restaurants so take your own refreshments.

This is a long walk and you may decide to finish at the tomb of Cecilia Metella, about 3km from the start point. Try to go on a Sunday, when the Via Appia is closed to traffic apart from buses and wedding parties.

Go straight through Porta San Sebastiano (➤ 63) and follow the road to the entrance to the Catacombs of San Callisto (➤ 37).

On the left is the church of Domine Quo Vadis, which has the imprints of Christ's feet, left when he appeared to St Peter who was trying to escape from Rome.

Bear right down Via Ardeatina, past the Catacombs of Domitilla to the Fosse Ardeatine.

This is now a moving memorial to the 335 Italians who were shot here by Nazis during World War II.

Follow Vicolo delle Sette Chiese back to the Via Appia and turn right at the Basilica San Sebastiano.

Opposite is the 4th-century tomb of Romulus (son of Emperor Maxentius) and the remains of Maxentius's stadium. Beyond this is the round tomb of Cecilia Metella, wife of a rich 1st-century BC Roman. Stop for lunch here or finish your walk.

From now on the traffic eases as the road, paved with its original vast, uneven cobblestones, cuts straight across the country. The cobbles are of Latium whitish lava stone. The route here is lined by the attractively crumbling tombs of ancient Romans. Along the stretch up to Via Erode Attico there are several modern villas, but beyond that the view gives way to farmland.

The walk finishes at the junction with Via del Casal Rotondo, where another massive round tomb has been converted into a farmhouse.

About half-way along this stretch are the remains of aqueducts and the complex of buildings (including a nyphaeum near the roadside) that made up the 2nd-century AD Villa of the Quintilli.

Turn left at Via del Casal Rotondo and walk until you reach Via Appia Nuova where you can take a bus back into the centre.

Via Appia Antica was built in 312 BC by Appius Claudius Caecus

PORTA SAN SEBASTIANO ✪

The best-preserved of Rome's ancient gateways, the Porto San Sebastiano, leading to the Via Appia Antica (► 62), was rebuilt in the 5th century AD. Today it houses a rather dry museum on the history of the Roman city walls, the highlight of which is a stretch of walkway along the top of the 3rd century AD Aurelian wall.

➕ 29D1
✉ Via di Porta San Sebastiano 18
☎ 06 7047 5284
🕐 Tue–Sat 9–7, Sun 9–1
🚌 218, 660 to Porta San Sebastiano
🎫 Moderate

PROTESTANT CEMETERY ✪

In fact this serene spot is called the non-Catholic rather than the Protestant cemetery but, in the first years after its establishment in 1738, most of its occupants were Protestant and the name has stuck. A map at the entrance will help you locate the final resting places of, among others, English poets Keats and Shelley, Julius, the son of German poet J W von Goethe, and Antonio Gramsci, the founder of the Italian Communist Party.

➕ 28C1
✉ Via Caio Cestio 6
☎ 06 574 1141
🕐 Mar–Sep, Thu–Tue 8–11:30, 3:20–5:30; Oct–Feb, 8–11:30, 2:20–4:30
🚌 57, 75, 175
🎫 Donation

SANT'AGOSTINO ✪✪

An important early Renaissance Roman church containing a sculpture of the pregnant Mary by Sansovino (1518–21), an altar with Bernini angels and a Byzantine Madonna. The main attractions are, however, the paintings by Raphael and Guercino and Caravaggio's beautiful *Madonna di Loreto* (painted in 1606, just before he had to flee Rome to escape a murder charge). Caravaggio's realistic portayal of biblical figures as poor people, usually (as here) illuminated in the foreground and forming a strong diagonal across the picture, were criticised for lack of decorum because of their dirty feet, ripped clothes and perhaps too-human Madonna.

➕ 28C3
✉ Piazza S. Agostino
🕐 8–12, 4.30–7.30
🚌 70, 81, 87, 115, 186, 492, 628 to Corso del Rinascimento

Did you know ?

Sant'Agostino was where many of Rome's most sought-after courtesans came to worship, attracting a large following of male admirers. For an attractive, go-getting Renaissance girl, life as the kept woman of a Roman aristocratic (or even a senior church man; many of the popes' so-called nephews were really their sons) could lead to riches and a successful career (like the mother of Lucrezia and Cesare Borgia who bought and ran three hotels).

SANT'ANDREA AL QUIRINALE ✪✪

A theatrical Bernini gem (1628–70) decorated in pink marble. The portico beckons and the interior embraces soothingly. The oval space (imposed by site restrictions), the short distance between entrance and altar, the gold ceiling, dark chapels and four massive richly veined columns all combine to pull one's gaze to the altar and Cortese's marble-framed *Martyrdom* borne by angels. On the pediment above, St Andrew soars to heaven, while garlanded *putti* perch and fishermen recline. The architectural expression of Bernini's sculptural ideals, it was his personal favourite, built for no payment. Also worth noting are the walnut-lined sacristy and chapels of St Stanislao (paintings by Sebastiano del Pozzo, statues by Legros).

➕ 29D3
✉ Via del Quirinale 29
🕐 10–12, 4–7
🚌 71, 115, 116 to Via Milano; 57, 64, 65, 70, 75, 170 to Via Nazionale

SANT'ANDREA DELLA VALLE ✪

Another great Counter-Reformatory church to put Protestantism on the defensive and accommodate yet another new Order (the Theatines, founded in 1524). Designed by Della Porta (1591), it has a superb and imposing travertine façade (Rainaldi, 1655–63) and Carlo Maderno's impressive dome (1622), which is second only to that of St Peter's and also contains one of the church's important baroque fresco cycles. Other frescoes, by competitors Lanfranco and Domenichino in the dome, and Domenichino's *Scenes from the Life and Death of St Andrew* in the apse, have been recently restored. Opera fans note that this is where the opening scene of Puccini's *Tosca* takes place.

SAN CARLO ALLE QUATTRO FONTANE ✪✪

Restored recently, this was Borromini's first major work (1638) after a long apprenticeship under Maderno. It is

difficult for modern eyes to appreciate the revolutionary quality of this tortured man's work. He overturned the Renaissance assumptions that architecture was based on the proportions of the human body, designing it instead around geometric units. The manipulation of the minuscule space is ingenious, not least in the swiftly shrinking coffers of the honeycombed dome, which give an illusion of size. The changing rhythms inside are also present on the façade, Borromini's last work (1667). The three bays of the lower half read concave-convex-concave while those above are all concave.

Borromini made the most of a restricted space when he designed the church of San Carlo alle Quattro Fontane

SANTA CECILIA IN TRASTEVERE ✪✪

Approached through a delightful courtyard, this church contains one of the most beautiful baroque sculptures in Rome (Stefano Maderno, 1599), showing a tiny Saint Cecilia, the patron saint of music. Supposedly in the position of her nasty death (it took her three days to die), her head poignantly turns from our gaze. There are also the great Cavallini's frescoes of the *Last Judgement* (1293), painted in beautifully soft powdery blues, greens and pinks of the trumpeting angels' wings. Underneath the church, the remains of a Roman house and shops, including a mosaic, can still be seen.

SAN CLEMENTE (► 23 TOP TEN)

SANTA CROCE IN GERUSALEMME ✪

This church bursts with relics; indeed it was built (1144) for that very purpose. In the Chapel of the Relics are pieces of the True Cross and thorns from Christ's Crown brought to Rome by the Empress Helena in 320, whose crypt is built on soil from Mount Golgotha. The chapel contains some wonderfully ornamental mosaics showing scenes decked with flowers and birds.

✚ 29E2
⊠ Piazza di Santa Croce in Gerusalemme
🕐 Apr–Sep, 6–12:30, 3:30–7:30; Oct–Mar, 6–12:30, 3:30–6:30
🚌 9 and trams 13, 30B to Piazza Santa Croce in Gerusalemme

SAN FRANCESCO A RIPA ✪

A 13th-century monastery was built on the site of an inn where St Francis of Assisi supposedly stayed but the present church is baroque (1692, by de' Rossi, working under Bernini). Architecturally uninteresting, it does however house one of Bernini's most splendid works (*The Blessed Ludovica Albertoni*, 1674). Framed in the last left chapel, she is best approached head-on from the nave. Depicted in feverish death throes after her life of good works, the agonised writhings of the deeply cut white folds of her clothes create a powerful impact. The textures of hair, skin or the bed are not differentiated and the whiteness is intensified by the dark foreground drapes, close enough to touch.

✚ 28B2
⊠ Piazza San Francesco d'Assisi
🕐 7–12, 4–7
🚌 40, 64, 70, 71, 492 to Largo Argentina then tram 8 to Viale Trastevere

SAN GIOVANNI IN LATERANO ✪✪✪

This was the home of the papacy from Constantine until 1305, and is the present cathedral of Rome. In short, it is an important place. The early buildings suffered from fire and neglect after the Pope's exile to Avignon and the subsequent move to the Vatican, and the present-day San Giovanni dates from the baroque: including Fontana's palace and portico (1585), Gallei's façade and Borromini's nave (1650), which incorporates the columns of the original basilica inside a new and vigorous structure, creating niches for figures of the Apostles. Look out for the 5th-century mosaics in the baptistery apse and the bronze door (1190) of the chapel of St John the Evangelist. The baptistery was damaged by a bomb in 1993.

✚ 29E2
⊠ Piazza di San Giovanni in Laterano
🕐 Apr–Sep, 7–7; Oct–Mar, 7–6
Ⓜ San Giovanni
🚌 16, 81, 85, 87, 218, 650, 714, 715 to Piazza di San Giovanni in Laterano

Borromini's nave within Rome's cathedral church

Andrea Pozzo's beautiful and fantastic trompe l'oeil *ceiling in Sant'Ignazio di Layola depicts the saint's entry into Paradise*

🕂 29D2
✉ Piazza di San Gregorio Magno
🕐 9–1, 4–7
🚇 Circo Massimo
🚌 81, 175, 673 to Via di San Gregorio

SAN GREGORIO MAGNO ✪

Originally Gregory the Great's monastery (575), from where he set out to take Christianity to England, it is now a feast of baroque, with Soria's masterpiece of a façade (1629) sitting decorously at the top of a splendid flight of stairs. More interesting than the church interior is the (sadly neglected) adjacent Oratory. The first room contains the table (supported by 3rd-century carved griffins) from which Gregory was said to have fed 12 poor people daily. In the central chapel (dedicated to St Andrew) is the lovely misty-coloured fresco by Reni of *St Andrew Adoring the Cross* and Domenichino's even lovelier *Scourging*.

🕂 29D3
🕐 7:30–12:30
✉ Piazza di Sant'Ignazio
🚌 62, 81, 85, 95, 160, 175, 492, 628 to Via del Corso; 119 to Via del Seminario

SANT'IGNAZIO DI LOYOLA ✪

The interior of this second Jesuit church (Il Gesù, ➤ 43) is a late-baroque (1626–50) assault on the senses, epitomised by Jesuit artist, Andrea Pozzo's astonishing fresco in the nave – *Apotheosis of St Ignatius* (1691). An extraordinary feat of perspective, the *trompe l'oeil* architecture becomes indistinguishable from the real. The dome, too, is painted (find the spot, move and watch the perspective distort). Similarly sumptuous are St Aloysius' tomb with its lapis lazuli urn and the altar with Legros' relief sculpture (right transept 1698–9). The friezes are by one of the baroque period's finest, Algardi.

🕂 76A2
✉ Piazza San Lorenzo in Lucina
🕐 7:30–12:30
🚌 60, 62, 81, 85, 95, 160, 175, 492, 628 to Via del Corso

SAN LORENZO IN LUCINA ✪

St Lawrence suffered a gruesome martyrdom (258) by being roasted on the gridiron found in this church. It takes its name from Lucina, one of the Roman matrons who gave her house over to Christian worship, but was rebuilt for Pope Paschal II (c1100) with a Romanesque belltower and a cosmati portico of refreshing simplicity, carefully restored. Inside is Bernini's chapel.

A Walk from the Celian Hill

The green and peaceful Celian hill overlooks the Colosseum, and adjoins the Baths of Caracalla and the Circo Massimo.

Starting at San Gregorio Magno (➤ 66), turn right up Via di San Gregorio and take the first right, Clivo di Scauro which runs under the flying buttresses that support Santi Giovanni e Paolo (➤ 33), opposite are the studios of Canale 5 (one of Berlusconi's TV stations). Continue straight up Via di San Paolo della Croce, under the 1st-century AD Arch of Dolabella and past the gateway of San Tommaso in Formis.

San Tommaso in Formis has a 13th-century mosaic of Christ freeing a black and a white slave. To the left is the church of San Stefano Rotondo (➤ 74), and on the right is Santa Maria in Domnica (➤ 69); the fountain was erected in 1931 using a 16th-century sculpture of a boat. Next to the church is the entrance to Villa Celimontana park.

At the bottom of Via della Navicella bear right down Via Druso and turn right along Viale delle Terme di Caracalla, passing the baths (➤ 75) to reach Circo Massimo (➤ 39).

Rest on the grass and let your imagination drift back to the chariot races.

Turn left on Viale Aventino and take the first right up Via di Circo Massimo. Follow this to Piazzale Ugo La Malfa and take the second left, Via di Valle Murcia following it up to the top .

Here there is a small orange garden with views over Rome. Following Via di Santa Sabina you reach Santa Sabina (➤ 73) and Santi Bonifacio e Alessio with its 18th-century façade, cosmati doorway and belltower.

Continue straight to Piazza dei Cavalieri di Malta (➤ 57). Turning left just before the piazza down Via di Porta Lavernale will take you back down to Via Marmorata for buses, but first have lunch near Piramide.

Distance
4km

Time
2 hours without stops,
3 hours with

Start point
San Gregorio Magno
✚ 29D2
Ⓜ Circo Massimo
🚌 To Circo Massimo Piazza di Colosseo

End point
Via Marmorata
✚ 29C2
Ⓜ Ostiense
🚌 to Via Marmorata

Lunch
Taverna Cestia (££) (➤ 98).
✉ Viale Piramide Cestia 87
☎ 574 3754
🕐 Closed Mon
Ⓜ Piramide
🚌 13, 30, 75

SAN LUIGI DEI FRANCESI

Founded in 1518 by Cardinal Giulio de' Medici (later Pope Clement VII) this, the French national church, is worth visiting mainly for its paintings, including a *St Cecilia* by Domenichino (1616) and Reni. The *pièces de résistance* are, however, the works by Caravaggio, *The Calling of St Matthew* and *The Martyrdom of St Matthew* (1599), in the Contarelli chapel. Both exemplify the artist's use of artificial lighting which casts the backgrounds into deep darkness, focuses attention on the story's essential elements and moulds the remarkably everyday figures who dominate the foreground. This everyday quality was perceived as irreverent and the most notorious example, *St Matthew and the Angel* (1602), is above the altar (note the dirty feet).

SANTA MARIA DELLA CONCEZIONE

If you feel like contemplating immortality then visit this little church (1631–8), a Barberini initiative for the Capuchin monks. The sombre theme is spelt out on the tombstone of a Barberini ('here lie dust, ashes and nothing'), but reaches a climax in the musty odour of the bone-lined crypt where dead monks' remains decorate the ceiling and walls. In the church are two major baroque paintings, Pietro da Cortona's *Ananias Healing St Paul of Blindness*, (1631) and Caravaggio's *Meditating St Francis*.

SANTA MARIA IN COSMEDIN

The austere intimacy of this lovingly restored 12th-century basilica in the heart of ancient Rome houses beautiful cosmati works so characteristic of Roman churches of the period. The Cosmati (actually several families but grouped together because of the preponderance of the name Cosma) were builders and designers but are best remembered for their luscious decorations in marble and colourful mosaics. Examples can be seen here in the magnificent nave paving (1123), the raised choir, the paschal candlestick, the bishop's throne and, in particular, the beautiful *baldacchino* (1294). In the portico is the *Bocca della Verità* (mouth of truth) – legend has it that the mouth would bite the hand of he who lied – or more commonly she whose marital fidelity was questioned. In the sacristy are mosaics (706) from old St Peter's.

Beautiful mosaics within the equally lovely medieval church of Santa Maria in Cosmedin

SANTA MARIA IN DOMNICA ✪✪

A haven of calm, this lovely church was rebuilt (817–24) in honour of the Virgin (who takes pride of place in the delightful apse mosaic showing saints striding through meadows). It is also known as *'La Navicella'* on account of the 16th-century copy of a Roman boat in front of the entrance. The boat is a fountain, made from an ancient stone galley; this may have been an offering made by a safely returned traveller. Pope Leo X added the portico and the ceiling. The theme of journeying continues in the 12 images of great delicacy and simplicity on the 11th-century wooden ceiling (among which are the ark, the tree of life and, in the centre, the Medici coat of arms). There is a notable 9th-century mosaic in the apse, which was commissioned by Pope Paschal I. Some excavated Roman remains are exhibited under the altar.

➕ 29D2
✉ Piazza della Navicella
🕐 Apr–Sept, 9–12, 3:30–7; Oct–Mar, 9–12, 3:30–6
🚇 Colosseo
🚌 81, 673 to Via della Navicella

SANTA MARIA SOPRA MINERVA ✪✪✪

Bernini's engaging obelisk-bearing baby elephant (1667) sits in the piazza in front of this typically eclectic church (built in 1280, completed in 1500, modified in the 17th century). Inside there is many a fine work: Bernini's wind-blown richly coloured marble monument to Maria Raggi (1643) and another to G B Vigevano (1617); Michelangelo's *Redeemer with his Cross* (1520); and the rich and lavish Aldobrandini chapel (della Porta and C Maderna, 1600–5) once again bearing witness to important Roman families making their own mark on baroque Rome. The treats, however, are Renaissance, notably the stunning frescoes by Lippi. Saint Valentine was made the patron saint of lovers here in 1465.

➕ 28C3
✉ Piazza della Minerva
🕐 7–12, 4–7
🚌 40, 44, 46, 60, 662, 64, 70, 81, 87, 115, 186, 492, 710 to Largo di Torre Argentina

Bernini's highly unusual elephant statue in the middle of Piazza della Minerva

69

SANTA MARIA DEL POPOLO ✪✪✪

☩ 28C4

✉ Piazza del Popolo

◷ Mon–Sat 7–1, Sun, hol 8–1:30, 4:30–7

🚇 Flaminio

🚌 To Piazzale Flaminio

The church is bursting with masterpieces. Part of the façade and interior are by Bernini, whose *Habbakuk* and *Daniel* statues are cramped into small niches in the Renaissance Chigi chapel (Raphael, 1516) along with mosaics. An angel visits Habbakuk and Daniel is praying with arms outstretched. Caravaggio and Carracci, the two dominant forces of baroque painting, are together in the Cerasi chapel (left transept). Caravaggio's *Conversion of St Paul*, so dramatically foreshortened that he seems to fall off the canvas, and the strong diagonals of the *Crucifixion of St Peter* share the space with Carracci's *Assumption of the Virgin* (1601). Pinturicchio (c1485), whose work can be seen in the frescoes, is represented by paintings in the Della Rovere chapel.

The church is worth visiting for any one of these works; to have them all under one roof nestling against the Roman wall in this magnificent piazza is a treat indeed.

Below: *Santa Maria del Popolo's rich interior is crammed with works of art*

SANTA MARIA IN TRASTEVERE ✪✪✪

☩ 28B2

✉ Piazza Santa Maria in Trastevere

◷ 7–1, 4–7

🚌 8 to Viale Trastevere

The 12th-century mosaics on the façade create a magical backdrop to the piazza, the heart and hub of this characteristic quarter, particularly when illuminated. Inside the basilica, is the glorious expanse of gold of the apse mosaic. This is the oldest church in Rome dedicated to Mary (3rd and 4th centuries, rebuilt in the 12th), and she is represented with almost equal stature to Christ in the mosaic's upper panel (c1140) below a fan-like kaleido-

scopic design of luxuriant blue. In the panels below are a series of exquisitely delicate representations of her life (by Pietro Cavallini, working in the late 13th century). There is also a cosmati floor and a ceiling by Domenichino (1617).

SANTA MARIA DELLA VITTORIA ✪✪

You could be forgiven for leaving Santa Maria della Vittoria off a busy itinerary; its baroque façade and interior are not the best examples in Rome, despite having been worked on by the architects Maderno and Soria and containing paintings by Domenichino, Guercino and Reni. However, it does contain Bernini's Cornaro Chapel and his *Ecstasy of St Teresa*, one of the finest pieces of baroque sculpture, making the church well worth a detour. Recently restored, *St Teresa* embodies Bernini's ideas of capturing the dramatic moment, in this case the saint's religious ecstasy (erotic to modern perceptions) as the Cornaro cardinals watch down from the side chapel.

✚ 29D4
✉ Via XX Settembre 17
🕐 Sep to mid-Jul, 7:30–12, 4:30–7; mid-Jul to Aug, 7–10:30
Ⓜ Repubblica

SAN PIETRO (ST PETER'S) (► 26, TOP TEN)

SAN PIETRO IN MONTORIO ✪✪

In the church is Bernini's Raimondi chapel, an important precursor to the Cornaro chapel (► Santa Maria della Vittoria, above) for its lighting effects. More significant is Bramante's *tempietto* ('little temple') in the courtyard of the adjoining monastery (1502), a seminal work in the history of architecture. Its perfectly proportioned simplicity and dignity, so in keeping with the commemoration of the (alleged) spot of Peter's crucifixion, expresses the Renaissance ideals of emulating classical architecture.

✚ 28B2
✉ Piazza San Pietro in Montorio
🕐 9–12, 4–6
🚌 41 to Gianicolo

SAN PIETRO IN VINCOLI ✪✪

To appreciate Michelangelo's *Moses* without jostling for position in front of the memorial to Julius II, make an early start. Flanked by Leah and Rachel (ironically representing contemplation), he remains remarkably impervious to the clicking cameras and rustling guidebooks, his gaze reaching out to some indeterminate spot across the nave, his hands sagaciously pulling back his abundant beard. Sculpted from a single piece of Carrara marble between 1513 and 1516, Moses is built on a large scale with enormous legs weighing him down and exquisitely moulded musculature; he is a massive expression of power and strength. Nearby, under the altar, lie St Peter's chains.

✚ 29D3
✉ Piazza San Pietro in Vincoli
🕐 7:30–12:30, 3:30–6
Ⓜ Cavour, Colosseo
🚌 75 to Via Cavour

Tradition has it that Santa Pudenziana stands on the site where St Peter once lived

🚇 29D3
✉ Via di S. Prassede
🕐 7–12, 4–6:30
🚉 Termini
🚌 16, 70, 71, 75, 590 to Santa Maria Maggiore

SANTA PRASSEDE ✪✪

Santa Prassede has mosaics unrivalled in medieval Rome. The figure of Christ dominates the vault, flanked by saints and Pope Paschal I (who built the church in 817–24), distinguished by his square halo of the living. The apse mosaics are rich in symbols: the phoenix (resurrection), the eagle, ox, angel and lion (the evangelists) and the four rivers of Eden (earthly paradise). The glimmering intricacy of mosaics can be enjoyed up close in the small, enchanting side Chapel of St Zeno. Behind the altar the saint deposits martyrs' blood and relics down the well beneath the nave. Worth noting is a bust of Monsignor Giovanni Battista Santoni carved by Bernini when a teenager.

🚇 29D3
✉ Via Urbana
🕐 Mon–Sat 8–12, 3–6, Sun 9–12, 3–6
🚉 Termini, Via Cavour
🚌 16, 70, 71, 75 to Piazza dell'Esquilino

SANTA PUDENZIANA ✪✪

The early Christian Basilica (401–17) was erected over ancient Roman baths and a house but tradition supposes this to be the site of the oldest church in Rome (AD 145). It has seen many changes over the centuries; witness the baroque opulence of the Caetani chapel, through which you descend to reach the ancient remains (mornings only; ask). The main impact, comes from the stunning 4th-century apse mosaics set in the nave's serene context.

SANTI QUATTRO CORONATI ★

Make sure you ask to visit the Oratory of St Silvester with its delightful frescoes (1246), *Scenes from the Life of Constantine*, situated in the adjoining convent. In soothing faded colours, and proof of how persistent was the influence of Byzantine art in Rome, you can see poor, spotty Constantine being cured of the pox by Pope Silvester. On the ceiling is a unique cross of five majolica plates. The Chapel of Santa Barbara has remains of medieval frescoes, and there is a garden in the inner courtyard. The church of Santi Quattro Coronati (Four Crowned Saints) has a typically long and complicated history; originally 4th-century, it was rebuilt in the 12th, as you can see from the belltower and cosmati paving. It more resembles a castle than a church.

29D2
Via dei Santi Quattro Coronati 20
9:30–12, 4:30–6
13, 15, 30, 85, 118 to Via San Giovanni in Laterano

SANTA SABINA ★★

The light-bathed interior of this perfect, serene early Christian basilica was built for Peter of Illyria (422–32), the belltower and cloisters were added in 1218 when the church was given to St Dominic and his newly formed order. Dominic's orange tree can be peeked at through a small gap in the portico. The church is named after the Roman Sabina martyred in Hadrian's time. Inside, the beautifully proportioned antique columns with their delicately carved Corinthian capitals support the nave arcading and 5th-century frieze. Unfortunately, the 5th-century mosaics on the apse and arch have not survived; the fresco reproductions are 15th-century. There is also a cosmati choir.

28C2
Piazza Pietro d'Illiria 1
7–12:20, 3:30–7
95, 713, 716 to Lungotevere Aventino

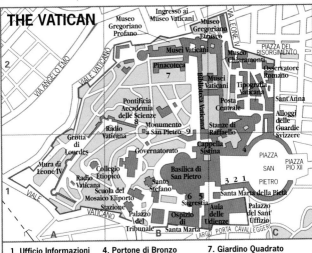

THE VATICAN

1. Ufficio Informazioni
2. Ufficio Postale
3. Arco delle Campane
4. Portone di Bronzo
5. Ufficio Scavi
6. Museo Storico Artistico
7. Giardino Quadrato
8. Fontana dell'Aquilone
9. Fontana del Sacramento

29D2
Via di Santa Stefano 7
9–1
81, 673 to Via della Navicella

SANTO STEFANO ROTONDO ✪

Beset by the usual problems of funding, Santo Stefano (one of the oldest round churches in Rome, c470) is in a constant state of restoration. Originally, the outer walls were further out, with circular and cross-shaped windows, and there were eight entrances. No evidence of an altar has been found (the present one is 13th-century); the two central columns supporting the lofty white-washed dome are also later additions. To the left of the present-day entrance a section of the original flooring has been painstakingly recreated using excavated marble fragments. Faded representations of gruesome martyrdoms (by Pomerancio and others c1600) adorn the walls.

SISTINE CHAPEL AND THE VATICAN MUSEUMS (➤ 24, TOP TEN)

28C2
Via del Teatro di Marcello
81, 95, 160, 628, 713, 716 to Via del Teatro di Marcello

TEATRO DI MARCELLO ✪✪✪

Here 2,000 years of Roman history can be seen at a glance. The lower part of the multi-levelled and many-styled building comprises the surviving two levels of a three-storey theatre that Julius Caesar started. Augustus finished the theatre in the 1st century BC and named it after one of his nephews. The elegant 16th-century palace, dramatically built on top of these crumbling remains (which served as, among other uses, a medieval fortress) and now divided into luxury apartments, was built by Baldassarre Peruzzi. The strange, reddish coloured protuberance stuck on the southern end is a 1930s Fascist addition, supposedly in keeping with the style of the theatre. To the north are three delicate Corinthian columns, part of a Temple of Apollo which was rebuilt in the 1st century BC. In summer, classical music concerts are held outside the theatre (➤ 114).

Above: *the Temple of Vesta;*
Right: *Terme di Caracalla*

TEMPI DI VESTA E DELLA FORTUNA VIRILIS ⭐⭐

Neither of these photogenic, small but perfectly formed temples have anything to do with Vesta or *Fortuna Virilis* (manly fortune). The round one, which dates from the 1st century BC and is the same shape as the temple of Vesta in the Forum (▶ 22), was dedicated to Hercules. The rectangular one, dating from the 2nd century BC, was dedicated to Portunus, the god of harbours; this was the port area of ancient Rome. Across the piazza from the temples is the 4th-century double arch of Janus, named after the two-headed guardian of the underworld.

🚩 28C2
✉ Piazza della Bocca della Verità
🚌 81, 95, 160, 628, 713, 716 to Piazza della Bocca della Verità

TERME DI CARACALLA ⭐⭐⭐

Ancient Romans did not go to the baths just to keep clean but to relax, meet each other, discuss politics, exercise and even study. Even bathing itself was not merely a soak in a tub; the Romans started off with a sauna, followed by a scrape down, a hot bath, a tepid bath and, finally, a dive into the cold bath. The serene ruins of the baths that Caracalla built in the 3rd century AD include remains of each of these types of bath as well as gyms, a library and a complicated underfloor heating system. They are used for summer outdoor opera performances (▶ 114).

🚩 29D1
✉ Via delle Terme di Caracalla 52
☎ 06 575 8626
🕐 Tue–Sat 9 to 2 hours before sunset, Sun–Mon 9–1
🚇 Circo Massimo
🚌 160, 613, 628, 714
♿ Few
💶 Moderate

28B1

Area between Via
Marmorata and
Lungotevere Testaccio

95, 716 to Via
Marmorata; 713 to
Lungotevere Testaccio

*Exclusive shopping on
the Via Condotti*

TESTACCIO ✪

Although well-known to Romans, who flock to its traditional restaurants and less-traditional nightclubs in the
evenings, the Testaccio area is off the main tourist track.
Most of its buildings are tall, courtyarded residential
blocks, dating from the end of the 19th century and
designed to include schools, crèches and shops, but it is
the area around Monte Testaccio that sees the action,
especially at night and during the summer (➤ 114–15).
The *monte* is made up of millions of broken *amphorae*,
dumped here by ancient Roman dockers when this was
the port area where ships unloaded their cargo, including

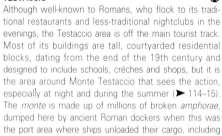

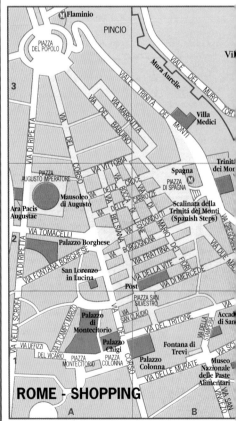

ROME - SHOPPING

the oil that was transported in these clay pots. Opposite the hill is the old *mattatoio* – the most sophisticated abattoir in Europe when it opened in 1891 – now used for concerts, art exhibitions and other cultural events.

VIA CONDOTTI ✪

Usually packed with well-heeled fashion victims and tourists, this elegant street is the heart of designer Rome, and most of the big Italian names have shops here or on the adjoining streets (▶ 108). It runs from Via del Corso to Piazza di Spagna and has an excellent view of the Spanish Steps. Keats and Liszt visited Caffè Greco at number 86.

➕ 76B2
✉ Via Condotti
Ⓜ Spagna
🚌 81, 90, 90b, 119 to Via Condotti

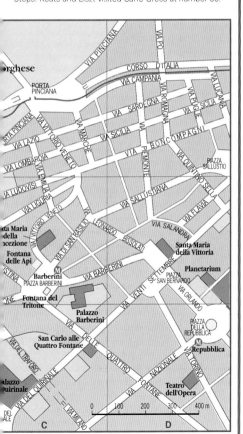

From high above, the designer delights of the Via Condotti are as yet unseen

Below: *the Sale delle Prospettive, and (inset) Raphael's fresco of Cupid, Villa Farnesina;*
Right: *view across rooftops to St Peter's*

VILLA FARNESINA

Baldassare Peruzzi built this delicate little villa in 1508 for the rich banker Agostino Chigi, who was also a patron of Raphael. Now it is used for temporary exhibitions although its otherwise empty rooms are also worth visiting for their spectacular frescoes by Raphael, whose *Triumph of Galatea* is on the ground floor along with the *Loggia di Psiche* which he designed, and Sodoma, whose seductive fresco of the *Marriage of Alexander the Great and Roxanne* is painted against a *trompe l'oeil* background of views of contemporary Rome.

VILLA GIULIA

This charming palace with its shady courtyards houses the national collection of Etruscan art, although it was originally built in 1550–5 as a summer residence for Pope Julius III. The central loggia and *nymphaeum*, decorated with frescoes and mosaics, were frequently copied in later 16th-century Italian villas.

The Etruscans arrived in Italy towards the end of the 8th century BC and settled between the Arno and the Tiber, the area known as Etruria (present day Lazio, Umbria and southern Tuscany). The objects unearthed from Etruscan tombs in the region bear witness to the sophistication of the civilisation. The highlight of the collection is the 6th-century BC terracotta sarcophagus of a husband and wife reclining on a divan (in room 9) found at the necropolis of Cerveteri. Have a look at some of the jewellery, and you will see that design has not necessarily changed all that much since.

✚	28B3
✉	Via della Lungara 230
☎	06 6880 1767
◷	Tue–Sat 9–1
🚌	280 to Lungotevere della Farnesina
♿	Free; moderate for temporary exhibitions

✚	28C5
✉	Piazzale di Villa Giulia 9
☎	06 322 6571
◷	Tue–Sat 9–7, Sun, hol 9–2
🚌	Trams 19, 30B to Piazza Thorwaldsen
♿	Few
♿	Moderate
↔	Galleria Nazionale d'Arte Moderna e Contemporanea (▶ 42)

Excursions from the City

Just as all roads lead to Rome, they also lead from it. To escape the chaos, crowds or summer heat dozens of destinations are within easy reach. Heading south are the fascinating excavations of Ostia Antica; further towards Naples are the sandy beaches of Sperlonga and Gaeta. To the southeast the Castelli Romani offer a fine combination of history and gastronomy, while to the northwest the tombs of the Etruscans are waiting to be discovered. Viterbo, to the north, offers medieval charm, hot springs and Renaissance architectural extravagances, while you can only marvel at the extensive ruins of Hadrian's villa to the northeast. Stopping for lunch at a local trattoria or selecting ingredients for a gourmet picnic is half the fun. But beware if you are driving, especially on Sundays. Romans are addicted to what they refer to as the *gita fuori porta* or day trip out of town and the traffic returning from these outings can be a nightmare.

'...[the Campagne Romana] is the aptest and fittest burial ground for the Dead City. So sad, so quiet, so secret in its covering up of great masses of ruin.'

CHARLES DICKENS
Pictures from Italy (1846)

ARICCIA: PALAZZO CHIGI

Alessandro Chigi was the pope who gave Rome its baroque face. This was his summer retreat, the centre-piece of Bernini's exercise in town-planning that is Ariccia. Sold by the Chigi family in the 1980s and opened to the public since 1999, his magnificent *palazzo* (built in 1672) has been beautifully restored to its original pale-blue colour. It is bursting with paintings and furniture from centuries of the family history. Particularly noteworthy are the pharmacy, with miniature portraits of the family from the 16th century onwards, and the *Salada Pranzo d'Estate*.

✚ Off map
✉ Piazza di Corte
☎ 06 933 0053
🕐 Tours: Tue–Fri 11:30, 4:30, 5:30, Sat–Sun 10–7 on the hour
🚍 COTRAL bus from Anagnina to Ariccia or from terminal to Albano Laziale then bus

BOMARZO ★

The *Sacro Bosco* or *Parco dei Mostri* (Park of Monsters) at Bomarzo near Viterbo was created in the mid-1500s by Prince Vicino Orsini. While other nobles were building refined villas and laying out Renaissance gardens, the prince had anonymous sculptors craft grotesque figures, including a life-size elephant crushing a Roman soldier with its trunk and a screaming face with a mouth big enough to hold several people. Inscriptions encourage today's visitors to 'eat, drink and be merry for after death there is no pleasure'. It was a favourite with Salvador Dali.

✚ Off map
✉ Sacro Bosco, 01020 Bomarzo (VT)
☎ (0761) 924029
🕐 Apr–Sep, 8:30–7; Oct–Mar, 8:30–5
🍴 Restaurant, bar
🚍 COTRAL bus from Saxa Rubra to Viterbo, then to Bomarzo.
💰 Expensive
🔁 Viterbo (➤ 90)

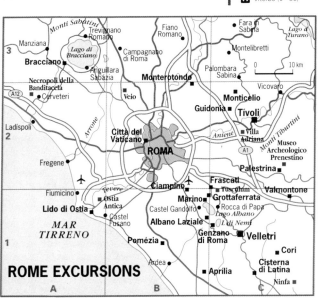

ROME EXCURSIONS

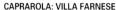

CAPRAROLA: VILLA FARNESE ✪

One of the high points of Italian Mannerism, the imposing Villa Farnese, built by Antonio di Sangallo the Younger for Pierluigi Farnese, dwarfs the little town of Caprarola. Cardinal Alessandro Farnese took up residence in 1559, hiring one of the most competent architects of the late Renaissance, Vignola, to modify his home. Retaining the original and unusual pentagonal floor plan, Vignola turned the entire town of Caprarola into a setting for the palace, raising and extending the approach road and burying the lower storeys of the existing houses.

The *piano nobile* is the only floor open to the public. It is approached by Vignola's monumental spiral staircase of stone columns and frescoes up which Alessandro Farnese

used to ride on his horse. Frescoes recording significant moments in the Farnese family history decorate all the rooms, except for the *Sala del Mappamondo*, where there are instead huge paintings of maps of the world (as it was known in the 16th century) and wonderful frescoes of constellations on the ceiling. The gardens outside are also worth a close look.

➕ Off map
✉ Piazza Farnese, 01032 Caprarola (VT)
☎ (0761) 646052
🕐 Apr–Sep, 8:45–6:45; Oct–Mar, 9–4
🚌 COTRAL bus from Saxa Rubra to Caprarola. **By car**: 80km SS2 bis (Cassia bis) from Rome, then SS2 to Sutri, then follow signs to Caprarola
♿ None 💵 Cheap

Villa Farnese

CERVETERI ✪✪

Founded by the Etruscans in the 8th century BC, ancient Caere was one of the great trading centres of the Mediterranean between the 7th and 5th centuries BC. In the **Banditaccia Necropolis**, a couple of kilometres from the main piazza of modern Cerveteri, the tombs of the inhabitants of the prosperous city are laid out in the form of a town, with streets and squares – a real city of the dead.

A map on sale at the entrance to the necropolis, which is set among Roman pines and cypress trees, is a useful guide to the tombs. Do not miss the 6th-century Tomba dei Capitelli carved from light volcanic rock to resemble Etruscan houses and the Tomba dei Rilievi decorated with painted reliefs of cooking utensils and other household objects. The Tomba degli Scudi e delle Sedie outside the main gate has chairs carved out of the tufo and unusual reliefs of shields decorating the walls.

The **Museo Nazionale di Cerveteri** in the town centre displays interesting pottery and sarcophagi from Cerveteri and the nearby port of Pyrgi, although most of the best discoveries are in the Vatican Museums (➤ 24) and Villa Giulia (➤ 78).

➕ 81A2

Banditaccia Necropolis/ Museo Nazionale di Cerveteri
☎ 06 994 0001
🕐 Banditaccia Necropolis: Tue–Sun 9 to 1 hour before sunset. Museo Nazionale di Cerveteri: Tue–Sun 8:30–7:30
🚌 COTRAL bus from Lepanto
🚉 From Termini, Tiburtina, Ostiense or Trastevere to Cerveteri-Ladispoli station (6km from town centre)
🚌 Local bus runs from main piazza in Cerveteri to necropolis in summer only. **By car**: 44km by A12 or Via Aurelia (SS1)
💵 Necropolis moderate; museum free

Etruria

Although little remains of Etruscan cities in the area of northern Lazio referred to as Etruria, many tombs, which contained reproductions of their occupants' luxuries and favourite things, have survived and give a fascinating insight into Etruscan civilisation. The Etruscans were clever, perhaps too clever for their own good. One historical account tells the story of an Etruscan man who set off for Gaul with his belongings and ample quantities of good wine. The precious nectar convinced the Gauls to come down to Italy, where they subsequently wiped out the Etruscan race.

Head out of Rome on the Via Aurelia (SS1), which joins the autostrada A12. After a visit to the necropolis of Cerveteri (➤ 82), continue north up the A12.

Civitavecchia, one of Rome's ports, is worth a detour. Established by Emperor Trajan in AD 106, the town regained importance as a papal stronghold in the 16th century, when Michelangelo designed the fortress.

Continuing on the A12 up the coast you reach Tarquinia.

This is thought to have been founded in the 12th century BC, an important economic and political centre for the Etruscans. The painted tombs at the necropolis of Monterozzi are a must. The Museo Nazionale di Tarquinia has a collection of artefacts.

Turn right onto a minor road after Tarquinia and head inland for about 20km until you reach Tuscania.

The Roman aqueduct at Tarquinia

This became a leading Etruscan city after the 4th century BC. Lovely sarcophagi are on display in the Museo Archeologico. However it is the post-Etruscan civilisation which makes an impression – especially the churches of San Pietro and Santa Maria Maggiore, built in the 8th century AD with 11th- and 12th-century additions.

Return to Rome by the same route or taking the Via Cassia (SS2) from Vetralla to Rome.

Distance
230km

Time
1 day

Start/end point
Rome
✚ 28C3

Lunch
Le Due Orfanelle (££)
✉ Via di Porta Tarquinia 11a, Tarquinia
☎ (0766) 856276
🕐 Closed Tue

⊞ 81C2
ℹ Frascati tourist office
(☎ 06 942 0331)

Villa Aldobrandini
✉ Piazzale Marconi, Frascati
☎ 06 942 2560
🕐 Mon–Fri 10–7
🚆 Train from Termini station, 30 min. **By car:** Via Tuscolana from Rome for about 25km
💷 Free (the tourist office in Piazzale Marconi issues passes to the garden of Villa Aldobrandini).

Renaissance villas of Frascati

FRASCATI ✪

Situated 25km from Rome, Frascati is the nearest of the Castelli Romani – the towns dotted along the volcanic Alban Hills. Frascati suffered severe damage during World War II, but many of the buildings have since been restored, including the cathedral of San Pietro in Piazza San Pietro and the church of the Gesù designed by Pietro da Cortona, which is decorated with fresco perspectives.

Frascati is renowned for both its white wine (this can be sampled fresh from the barrel in the numerous cellars around the town) and its Renaissance villas. The magnificent **Villa Aldobrandini**, designed by Giacomo della Porta between 1598 and 1603 for Cardinal Pietro Aldobrandini, a nephew of Pope Clement VIII, dominates the town. On a clear day the views of Rome from the terrace can be breathtaking.

Frascati, with other Castelli towns, was once part of the ancient city of Tusculum, which dates back as far as the 9th century BC. It was a favourite spot for Roman dignitaries, many of whom had villas there. The archaeological remains of Tusculum are scant: there is a Roman road leading up to the former city, the ruins of the villa of Emperor Tiberius and – best-preserved of all – a small amphitheatre now somewhat notorious after reports of black masses being held there. For directions refer to Castelli Romani drive (▶ 85).

Castelli Romani

The Castelli Romani are small towns which grew up in ancient times and developed during the Middle Ages along the slopes of the Alban Hills. The name probably comes from the palaces built there by popes and noble Roman families. Each has its own history and attractions.

From Frascati's Piazza G. Marconi, follow the signs to Tusculum (➤ 84).

Grottaferrata is 3km south of Frascati and is famous for its 11th-century abbey. Castelli wines are high on the list of popular Italian table wines. Even in Roman times they were regarded as 'unstable'. Today locals insist that the wine is better drunk on the spot. Test the theory by quaffing from the barrel in the wine shops in the towns.

Following route 215, you reach Marino, whose white wine is regarded as the region's best after Frascati. From Marino the scenic Via dei Laghi runs along the eastern rim of Lago Albano. Just after the lake, turn left on SS218 to Monte Cavo (the second highest of the Alban Hills) and Rocca di Papa, at 680m.

This is the highest of the Castelli towns and one of the most picturesque with its medieval quarter.

Return to Via dei Laghi until the turnoff on the right to Nemi. Nemi, positioned above the volcanic lake of the same name, is famous for its wild strawberries. It is an attractive place that gets busy at weekends. On the other side of Lake Nemi the panoramic SS7 continues to Genzano di Roma, Ariccia and Albano Laziale.

Ariccia is renowned for its main square ornamented by Bernini and for its *porchetta*, or stuffed roast pork. Albano Laziale has majestic Etruscan and Roman ruins.

From Albano Laziale take the picturesque Galleria di Sopra to Castel Gandolfo.

This is the summer residence of the Pope. He gives a blessing at 12:00 every Sunday, June to September.

Return to Rome on the Via Appia Antica.

Distance
90km

Time
Half a day

Start/end point
Rome
✚ 81C2

Lunch
Taberna Mamilius (££)
✉ Viale Balilla 1, Frascati
☎ 06 942 1559

🔲 81A1

☎ 06 5635 8099

🕐 Excavations Oct–Mar,
9–5; Apr–Sept, 9–6.
Museum 9–2

🍴 Il Monumento (££)
✉ Piazza Umberto I 18
☎ 06 565 0021

🕐 Closed Mon

🚇 Metro B to Magliana,
then the Ostia Lido train
to Ostia Antica. **By car**
25km. Via del Mare (SS8
bis) from Rome

👐 Moderate

*Visit Ostia Antica's
famously well-preserved
Roman town for a good
idea of what life was like
in Italy BC*

OSTIA ANTICA   ✪✪✪

Founded at the mouth of the river Tiber by the Romans in
the 4th century BC, Ostia Antica was the port of ancient
Rome. Populated by merchants and sailors, the city was a
strategically important centre of defence and trade until its
decline in the 4th century AD.

After Pompeii and Herculaneum, Ostia Antica is the
best-preserved Roman town in Italy. Its park-like setting is
a refreshing change from the chaos of Rome, and should
be enjoyed at a leisurely pace. Allow a good few hours to
explore the **excavations** which are as fascinating (if not
quite so grand) as those at the Roman Forum and give a
good impression of what day-to-day life in a working
Roman town was like.

The ruins span both sides of the kilometre-long main
street, the Decumanus Maximus, from the Porta Romana
to the Porta Marina at the other end (which once opened
on to the seafront). On the right just after the Porta
Romana are the Terme di Nettuno (baths of Neptune), best
viewed by climbing the stone stairs at the front. Further on
is the impressive amphitheatre which could hold 2,700
people. It was restored in 1927 and is used as a theatre in
summer (➤ 113). Behind the theatre is the town's
commercial centre, Piazzale delle Corporazioni, surrounded
by offices and shops with decorative mosaics announcing
the trades practised by each business.

Returning to the Decumanus Maximus, the ruins of the forum are to the left. Off to the right are the remains of some *horrea* (warehouses) that once stood all over the city. Also on the right is the well-preserved Casa di Diana and the *Thermopilium*, a Roman bar complete with a marble counter and frescoes of the available fare. Just beyond, to the northeast, is the museum which houses statues, mosaics and other artefacts found at the site.

Before you leave, look at the medieval *borgo* (village) of Ostia, a stone's throw from the archaeological site, where there are some characteristic cottages which once housed workers from the nearby salt plains and a fortified castle built for future Pope Julius II in 1483–6.

SPERLONGA ✪

With its whitewashed houses and narrow streets, the popular resort town of Sperlonga, built on a high, rocky promontory on the coast south of Terracina, is possibly more Greek than Italian in feel. Cars are banned from the old centre, which is made up of winding alleys and stone stairways. In the summer the spectacular beach is filled with wealthy Romans vying for a place in the front row of the beach-umbrella/sunbed operations (there is a small stretch of non-paying public beach but this seems to get smaller every year). Food and drink can be bought from the many beachside bars.

The archaeological museum located 2km from the town displays artefacts found among the ruins of the nearby villa of Emperor Tiberius, including reconstructions of larger-than-life-size sculpture groups illustrating the adventures of Ulysses, erected between AD 4 and 26 for Tiberius in his nearby cliff-face grotto.

Picturesque Sperlonga has a harbour as well as a very popular beach

➕ Off map
🍴 Lido da Rocco (£–££)
  ✉ Via Spiaggia Angelo 22 ☎ (0771) 54493
🚉 Naples train from Termini station to Fondi
🚌 Local bus to Sperlonga from Fondi should coincide with the train. Taxis also available. The return bus leaves from the central piazza at the top of the hill. **By car**: 120km. Take the SS148 south out of Rome (follow signs to Latina and Terracina). From Terracina take the SS213 to Sperlonga

The delightful grounds of Tivoli's Villa d'Este offer respite from the summer heat

TIVOLI

Tivoli was a country retreat for Roman patricians and a summer playground for the monied classes during the Renaissance. The town has long been famous for its Travertine marble and the quarries that line the road from Rome testify to this continuing flourishing trade. Easily reached by car or public transport, Tivoli is one of the most popular day trips from Rome. The Villa d'Este and Villa Adriana are the best-known sights, but it is worth having a look at the Rocca Pia, a 15th-century castle built by Pope Pius II at the top of the town, and wandering around the labyrinthine streets of the historical centre, stopping at the Romanesque church of San Silvestro (where there are some interesting early medieval frescoes) and the 17th-century cathedral of San Lorenzo.

There is a sense of faded splendour about the Renaissance pleasure palace **Villa d'Este** created in 1550 by Cardinal Ippolito d'Este, grandson of Borgia Pope Alexander VI. Some of the remaining Mannerist frescoes in the villa have recently been restored and deserve a look, but the residence is totally upstaged by the gardens – an almost entirely symmetrical series of terraces, shady pathways and spectacular fountains, powered solely by gravitational force and including one that once played the organ and another that imitated the call of birds. Sadly neither of these are functional today, but you can still get a sense of the fantastic creation that the garden once was, and there are delightful features such as the long terrace of grotesque heads, all spouting water, and the Rometta fountain (on the far left going down the terraces) which has reproductions of Rome's major buildings. From 1865 to 1886 the villa was home to Franz Liszt and inspired his *Fountains of the Villa d'Este*.

The waterfalls and gardens of Tivoli's **Villa Gregoriana** were created when Pope Gregory XVI diverted the flow of the Aniene river to put an end to the periodic flooding in the area. There are two main waterfalls: the large Grande Cascata on the far side and a smaller one at the neck of the gorge, designed by Bernini. Shady paths surrounded by lush vegetation wind down to various viewpoints over the waterfalls and across to two exceptionally well-preserved Roman temples, the circular Temple of Vesta and the rectangular Temple of the Sibyl, which date from the Republican era.

81C2

Cinque State (££)

✉ Largo Sant'Angelo

☎ (0774) 20281

Metro to Rebibbia, then COTRAL bus to Tivoli. Buses leave every 10 minutes (Mon–Sat), 15–20 minutes (Sun). **By car:** 40km east of Rome on Via Tiburtina SS5 or Rome-L'Aquila autostrada A24

Villa d'Este

✉ Piazza Trento

☎ (0774) 312070

🕐 9 to 1 hour before sunset

✋ Moderate

Villa Gregoriana

✉ Largo S. Angelo

☎ (0774) 334522

🕐 Apr, 9:30–6; May–Aug, 10–7:30, Sep, 9:30–6:30, Oct–Mar, 9:30–4:30

✋ Cheap

VILLA ADRIANA ✪✪✪

Constructed between AD 118 and 134, Villa Adriana was the largest and most sumptuous villa ever built in the Roman Empire. It was the country palace of Emperor Hadrian and later used by other emperors. After the fall of the empire it was plundered for building materials. Many of its decorations were used to embellish the Villa d'Este.

A model near the entrance gives you some idea of the scale of the complex. The site is enormous and you will need several hours to see it properly. Hadrian travelled widely and was a keen architect, and parts of the villa were inspired by buildings he had seen around the world. The massive *Pecile*, through which you enter, was a reproduction of a building in Athens and the Canopus, on the far side of the site, is a copy of the sanctuary of Serapis near Alexandria, and the long canal of water, originally surrounded by Egyptian statues, reproducing the Nile.

Highlights include the fishpond (probably used less for keeping fish than for creating reflections and plays of light) encircled by an underground gallery where the emperor took his walks, the baths, and Hadrian's private retreat, the Teatro Marittimo, a small circular palace on an island in a pool, which could be reached only by a retractable bridge. There are *nymphaeums*, temples, barracks and a museum. Archaeologists have found features such as a heated bench with steam pipes under the sand, and a network of subterranean service passages for horses and carts.

✚ 81C2
⊠ Via di Villa Adriana, Tivoli
☎ (0774) 530203
🕐 Nov–Jan, 9–5; Feb, Oct, 9–6; Mar, Sept, 9–6:30; Apr, 9–7; May–Aug, 9–7:30. Tickets sold until one hour before closing
🍴 Villa Esedra (£) ⊠ Via di Villa Adriana 51 ☎ (0774) 534716 🕐 Closed Tue
🚌 32km. Local bus from Tivoli's Piazza Garibaldi to Villa Adriana. COTRAL bus can drop you on main road to Rome (1km to villa).
♿ Moderate

In its day, the Villa Adriana, built by Emperor Hadrian, was the most lavish of its kind

Off map

Richiastro (£) Via Della Marrocca 16–18
(0761) 223 609
Closed Mon–Wed, Sun eve
COTRAL bus from Saxa Rubra station to Viterbo.
From Termini station (also Tiburtina, Ostiense, Trastevere stations) to Viterbo (2 hours). **By car:** Cassia bis (SS2 bis) from Rome (1½ hours). Pay parking.

San Pellegrino, the oldest quarter of medieval Viterbo, is often used for film locations

VITERBO ✪✪✪

Founded by the Etruscans and later taken over by Rome, Viterbo developed into an important medieval centre and in the 13th century became the residence of the popes. Although badly bombed during World War II, it remains Lazio's best preserved medieval town and its historical quarter, San Pellegrino, is such a perfect architectural ensemble that it is often used as a movie set. The natural hot springs close by are an additional attraction.

From the rather oddly named but lovely Piazza della Morte (Death Square) a bridge leads over to Piazza San Lorenzo and the black-and-white striped cathedral of the same name which dates from the 12th century. Inside are magnificent cosmati tiled floors and the tomb of Pope John XXI, who died in 1277 when the floor of his room collapsed. Next door is the 13th-century Palazzo Papale. Have a peek at the 'new' roof. The original one was removed in 1271, during the first conclave in Viterbo, to speed up the election of the pope. The cardinals, slow to elect the new pontiff, were locked inside the palace, next the roof was removed and finally, in desperation, the cardinals were put on a starvation diet. It was 33 months before Gregory X was finally elected.

The pretty Romanesque church of Santa Maria Nuova, with its outdoor pulpit from which St Thomas Aquinas preached and its cloister at the back, is also worth a look, before you head up towards Piazza del Plebiscito, which is dominated by the 16th-century Palazzo Comunale. Stop for a rest in Piazza delle Erbe by the fountain or for refreshments at the 15th-century Caffè Schenardi.

Where To...

*Above: nightlife
Roman style
Right: documents inside the
Keats-Shelley Memorial House*

Rome

How Much will it Cost?

The price brackets used here are for a three-course meal for one without drinks or service – a half litre of house wine will often not make that much difference to the bill especially in cheaper places:

£ = L.30,000–40,000;
££ = L.40,000–65,000;
£££ = up to L.100,000.

The bill will usually include a small cover charge (about L.2,000 per person) and some restaurants add service (10–15 per cent); otherwise tipping is usually about 10 per cent.

Agata e Romeo (£££)

Near the Basilica of Santa Maria Maggiore, this intimate, elegant restaurant is renowned for its cosy and convivial atmosphere, its excellent Roman and southern Italian dishes, and equally a wine list that pays tribute to the quality of the food.

⊠ Via Carlo Alberto 45
☎ 06 446 5842 ⊕ Closed Sun
⊕ Vittorio Emanuele
⊟ 70, 71

Alberto Ciarla (£££)

The classic Rome restaurant for serious fish lovers – fresh fish in its stark simplicity or as a sublimely creative dish, accompanied by a perfect match from the extensive wine list. There are intimate candlelit tables, a dramatic red-and-black decor, and refined and impeccable service.

⊠ Piazza San Cosimato 40
☎ 06 581 8668 ⊕ Closed
Sun, lunch ⊟ 44, 75, 170, 181

Albistrò (££)

This is a central restaurant near Corso Vittorio to which you can flee after an overdose of the ubiquitous Roman cuisine. Swiss, oriental and regional Italian dishes are all prepared with ingenuity, subtle flavours and delicate combinations. An inspiration.

⊠ Via dei Banchi Vecchi 140a
☎ 06 686 5274 ⊕ Closed
Wed; Sun, Mon, Tue lunch
⊟ To Corso Vittorio Emanuele

Alfredo a Via Gabi (££)

Comfortable local trattoria with pavement tables for outside eating in summer. Traditional and innovative specialities from Rome and the Marches, Roman dishes, especially on Saturday. A family atmosphere and cordial, attentive service. Remember to book at weekends.

⊠ Via Gabi 36 ☎ 06 7720
6792 ⊕ Closed Tue ⊕ Re di
Roma ⊟ 4, 87

Al 34 (trentaquattro) (££)

Seasonal vegetables and herbs characterise the predominantly southern Italian fish and meat dishes of this very popular central restaurant. There is a comfortable, intimate atmosphere, and efficient service. Book to avoid inevitable disappointment in the evening.

⊠ Via Mario de' Fiori 34
☎ 06 679 5091 ⊕ Closed
Mon ⊕ Spagna ⊟ To Via
del Tritone

Augusto (£)

This historic Roman trattoria has characteristic paper-covered tables (outside in summer). Happy confusion reigns here and service may be slapdash but the Roman cooking is genuine. Go early to enjoy the best dishes.

⊠ Piazza de' Renzi 15
☎ 06 580 3798 ⊕ Closed Sun
⊟ To Piazza Sonnino

Il Bacaro (££)

A candle-lit romantic little restaurant especially popular with young people both for its atmosphere and its location (near the Pantheon). It is particularly appealing in summer with outside tables. Innovative Italian dishes and affable service.

⊠ Via degli Spagnoli 27
☎ 06 686 4110 ⊕ Closed
Sun, lunch in Winter
⊟ To Largo di Torre Argentina

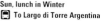

Da Baffetto (£)

Immensely popular central pizzeria, recognisable from afar due to the crowd jostling to get past the door. Service however is swift and efficient, the pizzas are well worth the wait. Not a place for lingering. Open late.

✉ **Via del Governo Vecchio 11** ☎ **06 686 1617** ⏰ **Closed Sun, lunch** 🚌 **To Corso Vittorio Emanuele**

Binario 4 (£)

A welcome arrival near the Colosseum: an updated version of the genuine local 'osteria'. There are carefully executed traditional dishes itemised daily on a strategically placed blackboard. Informal bonhomie. No rules for eating – have as little or as much as you like. Open late.

✉ **Via San Giovanni in Laterano 32** ☎ **06 700 5561** ⏰ **Always open** Ⓜ **Colosseo** 🚌 **To Piazza del Colosseo**

Cecilia Metella (££)

At the top of a winding drive, a shower of tables in a delightful garden setting, complete with fountain. Large, open-fire interior for winter. Cheerful, bustling waiters. Stress-free parking.

✉ **Via Appia Antica 12** ☎ **06 511 0213** ⏰ **Closed Mon** 🚌 **118**

Al Ceppo (££)

Skilfully recreated regional dishes from the Marches alongside creative variations on more local dishes are to be savoured in this elegant salon that has long enjoyed the exacting patronage of its local Parioli regulars. There is also a discerning wine list.

✉ **Via Panama 2** ☎ **06 841 9696** ⏰ **Closed Mon** 🚌 **To Piazza Ungheria**

Checchino dal 1887 (£££)

In the heart of Testaccio, this cool vaulted restaurant vaunts the experience of over 100 years. Quintessential Roman cuisine based on the once lowly offerings from the old slaughterhouse opposite. A superb natural wine cellar complements the meal.

✉ **Via di Monte Testaccio 30** ☎ **06 574 3816** ⏰ **Closed Sun eve, Mon, Christmas** Ⓜ **Piramide** 🚌 **13, 27, 30**

Ciak (££)

A rustic Tuscan bistro for lovers of game, roast meats and inimitable local specialities: checked tablecloths, engaging informal service, enthusiastic diners, friendly seating arrangements and an open grill all add to the enjoyment.

✉ **Vicolo del Cinque 21** ☎ **06 589 4774** ⏰ **Closed Mon, lunch** 🚌 **To Piazza Sonnino**

Colline Emiliane (££)

An old-fashioned family trattoria which adheres strictly to the well-established genuine traditions of the rich cuisine of the northern region of Emilia Romagna. Excellent homemade pasta, particularly *tortellini*, boiled meats and no frills.

✉ **Via degli Avignonesi 22** ☎ **06 481 7538** ⏰ **Closed Fri** Ⓜ **Barberini** 🚌 **To Piazza Barberini**

Il Convivio (£££)

A prime choice for a special gourmet occasion: creative cuisine spiced with a touch of genius and true professionalism. Both the well-balanced set menus and the *à la carte* dishes are tantalising in their range and variety; a comparable wine list.

✉ **Via dell'Orso 44** ☎ **06 686 9432** ⏰ **Closed Sun, Mon lunch** 🚌 **To Corso del Rinascimento**

Opening and Closing

In general, restaurants are open for lunch from about 12 until 3 and from about 8 until 11 for dinner. Most remain closed one day a week and many are closed two or more weeks in August and/or for up to a month in November or January, on Christmas day, Labour Day (1 May) and other public holidays.

93

What to Eat

A full Italian lunch or dinner starts with *antipasti* (raw and cooked vegetables, cold meats, sea-food) followed by the *primo* (first) course of pasta, rice or soup. *Secondi* are the main courses of meat or fish accompanied, or followed, by *contorni* (vegetables and salad). The meal finishes with *dolce* and coffee with digestive liqueurs. Although you do not have to eat your way through all of these, most restaurants expect you to have at least a couple of courses.

Ditirambo (££)

The two beamed rooms with tiled floors have the tranquillity of an old country inn; innovative Italian dishes are based on genuine ingredients and subtle combinations. Homemade bread, pasta and desserts; excellent (house) wine. Informative staff.

⊠ **Piazza della Cancelleria 74** ☎ **06 687 1626** ⓘ **Closed Mon** ▩ **To Corso Vittorio Emanuele**

Il Drappo (££)

The kitsch ceiling drapes (hence the name '*il drappo*') of this restaurant off Via Giulia envelop diners voluptuously together; the authentic Sardinian cuisine is a rare beacon in the capital. Set-price menu and booking obligatory.

⊠ **Vicolo del Malpasso 9** ☎ **06 687 7365** ⓘ **Closed Sun, lunch** ▩ **To Corso Vittorio Emanuele**

Enoteca Corsi (£)

An old-fashioned and comfortable central spot for a plain and simple lunch. No pretensions here – genuine Roman food, informal service and friendly diners eager to share their table space. Informal service. Adjoining wine shop also recommended.

⊠ **Via del Gesù 88** ☎ **06 679 0821** ⓘ **Closed Sun, eves** ▩ **To Largo di Torre Argentina**

Est! Est! Est! dei Fratelli Ricci (£)

Subdued but much loved central pizzeria with neither brashness nor pretensions. Diners will find simple wooden tables, minimal decor, excellent flat and crispy Roman pizzas, tap beer and regional Italian wines. An experience.

⊠ **Via Genova 32** ☎ **06 488 1107** ⓘ **Closed Mon, lunch** ▩ **Repubblica** ▩ **To Piazza della Repubblica**

Fiaschetteria Beltramme (££)

Try to get here early after shopping in the centre. A nostalgic survivor of past glories, this tiny trattoria is beginning to suffer from too much superstar visibility, so catch the lingering atmosphere. Share your table, jostle with the famous and enjoy genuine Roman cooking in suitably uninhibited cramped conditions.

⊠ **Via della Croce 39** ☎ **None** ⓘ **Closed Sun** ▩ **Spagna** ▩ **To Via del Corso**

Fornarina (££)

Dine romantically in summer in the ancient walled candlelit courtyard garden and bask in the atmosphere of the home of Raphael's famous mistress and model ('*La Fornarina*'). Almost as atmospheric in winter. Roman cuisine.

⊠ **Via di Porta Settimiana 8** ☎ **06 581 8284** ⓘ **Closed Mon** ▩ **To Lungotevere della Farnesina**

Da Gino (£)

Central, cheerful, chaotic, crowded and cheap! Politicians and journalists jostle for a seat to enjoy homemade pasta and each day's traditional dish: *gnocchi* and *ossobuco* (Thu), *baccalà* (Fri), *trippa* (Sat). Wonderful *tiramisù* has to be eaten to be believed.

⊠ **Vicolo Rosini 4** ☎ **06 687 3434** ⓘ **Closed Sun** ▩ **To Via del Corso**

Gioia mia (Pisciapiano) (£)

A useful spot after a hard day's shopping, offering menus for all palates and purses: from pizzas to full-blown meals. Noisy and chaotic but enjoyable nonetheless. (*Pisciapiano*, for those with linguistic curiosity, actually refers to a Tuscan wine with diuretic qualities, hence the emblematic cherub relieving himself.)

✉ **Via degli Avignonesi**
☎ **06 488 2784** 🕐 **Closed Sun**
🚇 **Barberini**
🚌 **To Piazza Barberini**

Girarrosto Toscano (£££)

This large, bustling restaurant is a sure culinary oasis in the residential area near St Peter's. Book to ensure your enjoyment of quality Tuscan T-bone steaks, mountain ham, homemade pasta, delicious bread and the company of other dedicated diners.

✉ **Via Germanico 58** ☎ **06 3972 5717** 🕐 **Closed Mon**
🚇 **Ottaviano** 🚌 **To Piazza del Risorgimento**

Grappolo d'Oro (£)

A stone's throw from Campo de' Fiori, this pleasant trattoria continues to offer typical basic Roman fare at prices that are more than reasonable for such a location. Discreet, cordial service and guaranteed satisfaction.

✉ **Piazza della Cancelleria 80**
☎ **06 686 4118** 🕐 **Closed Sun**
🚌 **To Corso Vittorio Emanuele**

Hostaria Romana (££)

Close to the Trevi Fountain and familiarly known to locals as 'Sergio and Ada'. Hot pizza bread, a wide variety of appetizers, great bowls of steaming pasta, fresh fish and Roman meat dishes ensure a dedicated and happy clientele. There are also inexpensive set menus.

✉ **Via del Boccaccio 1** ☎ **06 474 5284** 🕐 **Closed Sun** 🚌 **To Via del Corso**

L'Isola Felice (££)

Cheerful home-from-home tiny welcoming trattoria with good plain regional Italian cooking, based on skilful combinations of seasonal

products and unexpected individual touches. Delicious homemade desserts. Some tables outside in summer. Excellent wine list.

✉ **Vicolo del Leopardo 39a**
☎ **06 581 4738** 🕐 **Closed Sun, lunch** 🚌 **To Piazza Sonnino**

Ivo a Trastevere (£)

Go early to avoid the evening queue. Savour a classic Roman pizza and join the scores of contented customers who can say that they have eaten at this institution. Polluted tables outside for those who are non-environmentalists. Open late.

✉ **Via San Francesco a Ripa 158** ☎ **06 581 7082**
🕐 **Closed Tue, lunch**
🚌 **To Piazza Sonnino, Viale Trastevere**

Lorodinapoli (££)

This popular new Neapolitan restaurant is based on an astute winning formula: a concise lunch menu and an inspirational evening one, which changes every day according to available ingredients and the creativity of the chef. Essential to book ahead. Open late.

✉ **Via Fabio Massimo 101**
☎ **06 323 5790** 🕐 **Closed Sat lunch, Sun eve, Mon**
🚇 **Ottaviano** 🚌 **To Piazza del Risorgimento**

Da Lucia (£)

Catch the last glimpses of the fading splendours of one of old Trastevere's culinary historic spots. Genuine Roman dishes are traditionally and carefully prepared and served without undue ceremony, as is the wine. Sit outside in summer and take in the local atmosphere.

✉ **Vicolo del Mattonato 2b**
☎ **06 580 3601** 🕐 **Closed Mon, 2 weeks at Christmas**
🚌 **To Piazza Sonnino**

Piatti di Buon Ricordo

Some restaurants take part in the *piatto del buon ricordo* (literally, 'plate of good memory') scheme, in which anybody ordering the special dish of the house will be presented with a plate to take home with them. At Agata e Romeo, for example, the *piatto del buon ricordo* is *pasta e broccoli in brodo di arzilla* (pasta and broccoli).

Snacking

Rome has several eating alternatives if you are in a hurry or only want a snack. *Enoteche* (wine bars) often have cheeses, cold meats and sometimes pasta dishes to accompany their wine lists. *Birrerie* sell beer and basic dishes such as hamburgers. *Pizza al taglio* sell slices of freshly made pizza to take away. Bars have sandwiches and sometimes a *tavola calda*, with one or two hot *primi* and *secondi*. Finally, *alimentari* (grocers) fill rolls with whatever is in stock.

McDonald's (£)

The best of the chain, now spawning offspring throughout the city. There is something for everyone – an upstairs bar serving ice-cream and pastries and, in the spacious basement, a mouthwatering range of fresh mixed salads for the diet-conscious (alongside calorific desserts), as well as the usual US specials.

✉ Piazza di Spagna 46
☎ 06 6992 2400 🕒 Always open 🚇 Spagna 🚌 To Via del Tritone

Margutta Vegetariano (£)

A good vegetarian restaurant and a place to drop in, at any time of day, for a drink, a snack or a complete meal. Good selection of Mediterranean vegetable dishes and a recommended delicate *fritto misto*.

✉ Via Margutta 118
☎ 06 3600 1805 🕒 Always open 🚇 Flaminio 🚌 To Piazzale Flaminio

Le Maschere (££)

A rustic basement restaurant, glowing with wall masks, within a splendid 17th-century Roman palace. Almost impossible to resist the vast colourful display of fresh vegetable dishes and appetizers at the entrance. Fiery Calabrian cuisine and magnificent pizzas. The wines are predominantly Calabrian wines.

✉ Via Monte della Farina 29
☎ 06 687 9444 🕒 Closed Mon, lunch 🚌 To Largo di Torre Argentina

Trattoria Monti (££)

A delightful family-run local trattoria recommended for its carefully executed traditional dishes from the Marches and regular daily favourites: *gnocchi* on Thursday, *baccalà* on Friday, *trippa* on Saturday, baked lasagne (*vincisgrassi*) and

roasts on Sunday. Commendable wines. Booking advisable.

✉ Via di San Vito 13a
☎ 06 446 6573 🕒 Closed Tue 🚇 Termini 🚌 To Santa Maria Maggiore

Der Pallaro (£)

Democratic authentic Roman family-run restaurant near Campo de' Fiori with no ordering involved – each course of the changing daily menu is brought swiftly to your table. Some tables outside when the sun shines. Open late.

✉ Largo del Pallaro 15 ☎ 06 6880 1488 🕒 Closed Mon 🚌 To Corso Vittorio Emanuele

Panattoni (£)

A hugely popular Trastevere pizzeria nicknamed 'the coffin-maker' (*cassamortaro*) for its characteristic marble-topped tables. Watch the chef's flamboyant flipping of pizzas at the large oven inside, scramble for a pavement table in summer. Open late.

✉ Viale Trastevere 53 ☎ 06 580 0919 🕒 Closed Wed, lunc 🚌 To Viale Trastevere

Papà Baccus (££)

An eminently reliable welcoming restaurant in the often daunting Via Veneto area. From his native mountainous Tuscany, the owner offers traditional country soups, ham, salami, grilled meats and fish, homemade desserts. Informal service, seats outside in summer.

✉ Via Toscana 36 ☎ 06 427 2808 🕒 Closed Sat lunch, Sun 2 weeks at Christmas 🚇 Barberini 🚌 To Via Vittorio Veneto

Da Paris (££)

Satisfied customers return again and again to attest to the winning formula of Trastevere's prime Roman-

Jewish restaurant: unchanging traditional dishes and a sapient use of fresh ingredients. Delicate *vegetable fritto misto*, fresh fish. Small terrace in front, lofty rooms within. Well-selected wine list.

✉ **Piazza San Calisto 7a**
☎ **06 581 5378** 🕐 **Closed Sun eve, Mon** 🚋 **To Viale Trastevere**

Peccati di Gola (££)

Set in a scenic quiet piazza of Trastevere, and particularly atmospheric in summer, this elegant little restaurant (aptly named after culinary over-indulgence) specialises in Mediterranean and Calabrian fish dishes. Various reasonable set menus. Friendly, attentive service.

✉ **Piazza de' Ponziani 7a**
☎ **06 581 4529** 🕐 **Closed Mon** 🚋 **To Viale Trastevere**

Perilli a Testaccio (££)

A popular, noisy and crowded trattoria making no concessions to fashionable décor, thriving on its reputation for gargantuan portions of honest Roman specialities. Locals rub shoulders with the famous and everybody really enjoys themselves. Booking ahead is essential.

✉ **Via Marmorata 39**
☎ **06 574 2415** 🕐 **Closed Wed** Ⓜ **Piramide** 🚋 **To Via Marmorata**

Piperno (£££)

At the heart of the Jewish Ghetto, the name Piperno has been synonymous with the best (and not cheap) Roman-Jewish cuisine for over 100 years. Time really does seem to stand still in this restaurant: the old-fashioned decor is a sombre backdrop, the waiters exude an olde-worlde chivalry and the classic food is consistently genuine.

✉ **Monte de' Cenci 9**
☎ **06 6880 2772** 🕐 **Closed Sun eve, Mon** 🚋 **To Via Arenula, Lungotevere de' Cenci**

Pizzaré (£)

Worth a stop, especially at lunchtime, for true large-format Neapolitan pizzas in nearly 40 different combinations. Set menus at ludicrously low prices; also pasta, meat, salads and desserts.

✉ **Via di Ripetta 14**
☎ **06 321 1468** 🕐 **Closed Sun lunch** 🚋 **To Lungotevere in Augusta**

Trattoria Priscilla (£)

A useful place after trekking around the catacombs and one that is not hard on the pocket. Simple family-run trattoria offering classic Roman fare with no concessions to *haute cuisine* but happy to serve a plate of pasta and a glass of wine.

✉ **Via Appia Antica 68**
☎ **06 513 6379** 🕐 **Closed Sun** 🚌 **118**

Nel Regno di Re Ferdinando II (£££)

A new location in Testaccio for this highly acclaimed Neapolitan restaurant, serving all kinds of regional fish, meat and vegetable dishes and superb pizzas from the wood oven.

✉ **Via di Monte Testaccio 39**
☎ **06 578 3725** 🕐 **Closed Sun** Ⓜ **Piramide** 🚋 **To Via Marmorata**

Li Rioni (£)

An original street-like pizzeria, complete with tiled courtyard, streetlights and balconies. The atmosphere plus the excellent choice of pizzas have made it a local hot spot. Very popular so be prepared to queue.

✉ **Via Santissimi Quattro 24**
☎ **06 7045 0605** 🕐 **Closed Tue, lunch** 🚋 **To Piazza del Colosseo**

Pizzas

The best pizzas have a hint of charcoal around the edges. This is caused by being cooked in wood ovens (*forno a legna*), which create temperatures that seem unbearable in summer. Not all pizzas are the same; Roman ones have a thin, crisp base while, in Naples, pizzas come on a thick, bready base, which is more filling; *calzone*, a particularly appetite-satisfying option, are made from folded over pizza dough stuffed with the filling you choose.

Rome & Excursions from the City

Vegetarians

In Rome there is a dearth of restaurants catering exclusively to vegetarians but that should not stop you from eating well. Even if you do not eat any animal products at all, wherever you go you are likely to find a good selection of delicious meat-, fish- and egg-free pasta dishes, which you can follow with a selection of vegetables (contorni) or cheese.

Romolo nel Giardino della San Teodoro (££)

Stumble across this enticing and elegant little trattoria in its romantic setting and you will be treated to a memorable experience, especially in summer. Grilled meats, fresh fish and Roman specialities. Informal, welcoming. Good wines.

✉ Via dei Fienili 49 ☎ 06 678 0933 🕓 Always open 🚌 To Piazza Bocca della Verità

Sora Lella (££)

A legendary Roman institution on the enchanting Tiber Island, embued with the shades of Sora Lella, a charismatic Roman personality. The food is, naturally, Roman; the diners may be illustrious. Charming, informative service.

✉ Via del Ponte Quattro Capi 16 ☎ 06 686 1601 🕓 Closed Sun 🚌 To Lungotevere de'Cenci, Lungotevere Anguillare

Sora Margherita (£)

Little more than a hole in the wall, this tiny, unpretentious, sparse and spartan trattoria in the Jewish Ghetto merits a lunchtime stop for its few, selected daily dishes. Genuine home cooking (and fresh pasta) at mouth-watering prices.

✉ Piazza delle Cinque Scole 30 ☎ 06 686 4002 🕓 Closed Sat, Sun, eves 🚌 To Via Arenula, Lungotevere de' Cenci

La Tana del Grillo (££)

The northern region of Emilia, and Ferrara in particular, offers its inimitable hospitality in this relaxed and understated restaurant, where the customer is made to feel immediately at home and dishes are wholesome and comforting. Affable, attentive service.

✉ Via Alfieri 4 (ang. Via Merulana) ☎ 06 7045 3517 🕓 Closed Sun, Mon lunch 🚌 To Via Merulana

Taverna Angelica (££)

A restaurant near St Peter's for romantic, intimate candle-lit dining until the small hours. Creative regional cuisine, both fish and meat, excellent cheeses and imaginative desserts (with well-matched dessert wines by the glass). Courteous and efficient service.

✉ Piazza delle Vaschette 14a ☎ 06 687 4514 🕓 Closed Sat lunch, Sun Ⓜ Ottaviano 🚌 To Piazza del Risorgimento

Taverna Cestia (££)

A quality-for-money restaurant enjoying favour with many of the foreign residents working for the nearby UN agency. An extensive menu of Italian dishes, competently executed, together with crisp Roman pizzas. Terrace outside.

✉ Viale Piramide Cestia 67 ☎ 06 574 3754 🕓 Closed Mon Ⓜ Piramide 🚌 11, 13, 27, 30

Tito e Quirino Fazioli (£)

A consistently good bet in an area that is notorious for tourist traps. Just behind Piazza Navona, this capacious and good-value trattoria turns out a succession of inspirational fish dishes and a variety of luscious desserts. Worthy wine list.

✉ Via Santa Maria dell'Anima 8 ☎ 06 686 8100 🕓 Closed Sun, lunch in summer 🚌 To Corso Vittorio Emmanuele

La Zucca Magica (£)

Dulcis in fundo – a vegetarian restaurant patronised by non-vegetarians for the culinary delights that only a chef of genius can produce. Each dish is painstakingly described – vegetables will never seem the same again. Tiny, cosy bordering on kitsch, a jewel of a central eating place. Recommended for lunch (after 1PM).

⊠ **Via dei Barbieri 23** ☎ **06 683 3207** Ⓦ **Closed Sun, Mon**
🚇 **To Largo Vittorio Emanuele**

Bracciano
Trattoria del Castello (££)

Classic, local cuisine, adapting medieval recipes to create special fish and meat dishes. Homemade pasta and an extensive wine list.

⊠ **Piazza Mazzini 1** ☎ **06 9980 4339** Ⓦ **Closed Wed**

Frascati
Cacciani (£££)

Classic, consistently reliable spacious restaurant in the Castelli Romani with a large panoramic terrace from which to view Rome's urban conglomeration. Classic meat and fish dishes from Rome and Lazio. Try the regional white Frascati wine.

⊠ **Via A Diaz 13** ☎ **06 942 0378** Ⓦ **Closed Mon**

Taberna Mamilius (££)

Friendly, elegant atmosphere with touches of rusticity. The menu, of mainly local dishes, changes daily according to the best of the season's ingredients that are available.

⊠ **Viale Balilla 1, Frascati** ☎ **06 942 1559** Ⓦ **Closed Wed/Sun eve**

Ostia Antica
Il Monumento (££)

Simple, well-made fish and seafood dishes are the mainstay of this trattoria in the village near the ancient remains of Ostia. The house speciality, '*spaghetti monumento*', is a wonderful mix of seafood and prawns.

⊠ **Piazza Umberto I 18** ☎ **06 565 0021** Ⓦ **Closed Mon**

Sperlonga
Agli Archi (£££)

All the dishes at this little restaurant are delicious, from the *antipasto* of hot and cold seafood, to the homemade puddings. The menu changes daily to take advantages of that day's catches and *mozzarella di bufala* (produced in the area) is another highlight. There is a good-value wine list.

⊠ **Via Ottaviano 17** ☎ **(0771) 548300** Ⓦ **Closed Wed, except in Jul and Aug**

Villa Adriana
Villa Esedra (£)

The *antipasti* and *primi*, of risotto or home-made pasta, offer a range of dishes that are slightly out of the ordinary for a *trattoria*. *Secondi* and puddings are more standard but still pretty good. Take a table outside in summer.

⊠ **Via di Villa Adriana 51** ☎ **(0774) 534716** Ⓦ **Closed Tue**

Viterbo
Aquilanti (£££)

This huge restaurant, in a 17th-century building, has a range of traditional Viterbo dishes, such as *I lombrichelli all viterbese* and bean soup with wild chicory.

⊠ **Via del Santuario 4** ☎ **(0761) 341701** Ⓦ **Closed Tue, Sun eve**

Richiastro (£)

Traditional local dishes that you will not find in many other places, using simple ingredients such as bread with a spread made from eggs and peppers, lentil and chick-pea soups, and tripe.

⊠ **Via della Marrocca 16–18** ☎ **(0761) 223609** Ⓦ **Closed Mon–Wed, Sun eve**

What's in a Name?

In general, a *trattoria* is an unpretentious, family-run concern often with a regular clientele of local people who drop in when they do not want to cook for themselves. *Ristoranti* are usually more formal and expensive places for a special occasion. *Osterie* used to be the most basic of all, where simple dishes were washed down with jugs of local wine, but beware – recently the name has been adopted by some of the most expensive or touristy establishments.

Rome

Prices

Hotels in Rome are not cheap. The price brackets used here are for a double room – rooms in the mid and upper price ranges nearly always have private bathrooms. Those in the lower range do not always, but nearly all hotels will have at least a few rooms with private bathrooms.

£   = under L150,000;
££ = L150,000–230,000;
£££ = over L230,000.

Aberdeen (££)

This friendly 26-roomed hotel (all with bathrooms) lies opposite the Ministry of the Interior, two steps from Santa Maria Maggiore. It was refurbished in 1996. English, French and German spoken.

✉ Via Firenze 48 ☎ 06 482 3920 🚇 To Via Nazionale

Campo dei Fiori (££)

Situated in one of the loveliest quarters of the centre, this hotel (terrace overlooks Roman rooftops) is in a flaking ochre-coloured street. Pleasant decor and multi-lingual staff.

✉ Via del Biscione 6 ☎ 06 688 06865/687 6003 🚇 To Corso Vittorio, Largo Argentina

Campo Marzio (£)

If you want a no-frills place to rest your head then this low-cost family-run *pensione*, although a little drab, is clean and superbly situated two steps from parliament and the Pantheon.

✉ Piazza Campo Marzio 7 ☎ 06 688 01486 🚇 To Largo di Torre Argentina

Canova (£££)

Completely refurbished in the summer of 1996 this 3-star, comfortably appointed hotel is situated in a lovely, quiet and safe street near the station at Santa Maria Maggiore.

✉ Via Urbana 10/a ☎ 06 487 3314/481 9123 🚇 Cavour 🚇 To Via Cavour

Caravaggio (££)

The lovely wooden-framed door gives the impression of a private club and the atmosphere of this refurbished, centrally located hotel is as welcoming as you might expect .

✉ Via Palermo 73 ☎ 06 485 915/474 7363 🚇 Repubblica 🚇 To Via Nazionale

Della Conciliazione (££)

Situated in one of the lovely streets tucked away behind the Vatican. The rooms are a little small but they are pleasantly furnished. Friendly service from a multi-lingual staff.

✉ Via Borgo Pio 164 ☎ 06 686 7910/6880 1164 🚇 To Piazza del Risorgimento

Coppedè (££)

A recently refurbished small establishment a little out of the centre in the much sought-after residential area designed by the weird and wonderful architect from which the hotel takes its name. Excellent value for price category.

✉ Via Chiana 88 ☎ 06 854 9535/854 9535 🚇 To Via Po

Corot (££)

Right next to the station so perfectly placed for getting to all sights both in and out of town, this hotel offers comfortable rooms and a hospitable and multi-lingual staff.

✉ Via Marghera 15/17 ☎ 06 4470 0900/4470 0905 🚇 Termini 🚇 To Termini

Cosmopolita (££)

Large, marble-floored rooms, courteous English and French-speaking staff, located right in the centre (so ask for inward-facing rooms). All facilities. Buffet breakfast included.

✉ Via IV Novembre 114 ☎ 06 6994 1349 🚇 To Piazza Venezia

D'Inghilterra (£££)
A very classy place, situated in a most elegant area of the city. Over a century old it boasts former guests such as Hemingway and Liszt.

✉ Via Bocca di Leone 14
☎ 06 69 981/6992 2243
🚇 To Piazza San Silvestro

Eliana (££)
At the bottom end of the medium-price range, this 2-star hotel still offers great value for money. Not a great street to be on at night but a great jumping-off point for daytime sightseeing.

✉ Via Gioberti 30 ☎ 06 446 5392 🚇 Termini
🚇 To Termini

Elite (££)
A moderately priced, very comfortable small hotel in an expensive area. It also has air-conditioning, an important consideration in the centre in the summer.

✉ Via F. Crispi 49 ☎ 06 678 3083/679 1761 🚇 Barberini
🚇 To Via del Tritone

Emmaus (££)
This fourth-floor 25-roomed hotel (some of the rooms have a view of St Peter's dome) is excellent value for this category. It has satellite TV and, unusually, wheelchair access.

✉ Via delle Fornaci 23 ☎ 06 635 331 🚇 To Via Gregorio VII

Enrica (£)
This cheap hotel near Rome's student quarter is run by a friendly multi-lingual ex-sailor and his wife. It has its own lovely garden.

✉ Viale Castro Pretorio ☎ 06 445 3742 🚇 Castro Pretorio
🚇 To Via Castro Pretorio

Esquilino (££)
On the 'clean' side of the station, this lovingly refurbished hotel is run by two professional hoteliers. Some rooms look out at Santa Maria Maggiore but the courtyard is quieter.

✉ Piazza dell'Esquilino 29
☎ 06 474 3454 🚇 Termini
🚇 To Piazza dell'Esquilino

Excelsior (£££)
Probably the most prestigious hotel in Rome with a luxury and service reminiscent of the days before mass travel.

✉ Via Vittorio Veneto 125
☎ 06 47081 🚇 Barberini
🚇 To Vittorio Veneto

Fiorella (£)
Exceptional value on Rome's elegant antiques street. It is small (book early) and the bathrooms are shared; rooms spotless and airy.

✉ Via del Babuino 196 ☎ 06 361 0597 🚇 Spagna 🚇 To Via del Corso

Firenze (££)
Completely restored at the end of 1995, on the first floor of a chic but busy street (near the Spanish Steps) so get a courtyard room.

✉ Via Due Macelli 106 ☎ 06 679 7240/678 5636 🚇 Barberini
🚇 To Via del Tritone

Grifo (££)
Tunisian family-run establishment, located in a lovely street in a quiet enclave near the Colosseum. Some rooms have delightful private terraces. Also available is a self-catering option on the top floor.

✉ Via del Boschetto 144
☎ 06 487 1395 🚇 To Via Nazionale

Hassler Villa Medici (£££)
One of the grandest old-style luxury hotels in the heart of the most elegant part of the centre with a view to die for from the elegant roof terrace and restaurant.

✉ Piazza Trinità dei Monti 6
☎ 06 678 2651/6994 1607
🚇 Spagna 🚇 To Via del Tritone

Booking
There are some 700 hotels in Rome but early booking is still advisable. Even the most modest places may want a telephone booking backed up by a deposit (a credit card will usually, but not always, be enough). If you do book, the local EPT tourist offices will help. There is an office in the centre (Via Parigi, 5; ☎ 06 4889 9253), at the station (☎ 06 487 1270) and at Fiumicino airport (☎ 06 6595 6074) with multi-lingual staff.

Rome & Excursions from the City

Special Needs

Italian culture and society may not accommodate special requirements formally, but the flexibility and initiative of the people means you could encounter extraordinary gestures of generosity (alternatively, you may find your path irremediably blocked). For example, hotels with no night porter often provide a key for guests who want to stay out late; those without breakfast may miraculously produce coffee. Unfortunately, the nature of Roman building does not lend itself to wheelchairs, but, whatever the official line, check with the individual establishment first.

Madrid (££)

At the top end of the moderate-price category in an expensive area, this 26-roomed hotel has all the amenities and a delightful inside courtyard-terrace.

✉ **Via Mario de' Fiori 89**
☎ **06 699 1510/679 1653**
🚌 **To Piazza San Silvestro**

Manara (£)

Very basic, also very cheap, with the distinct advantage of being located in lovely Trastevere, one of the best places to be of an evening.

✉ **Via Luciano Manara 25**
☎ **06 581 4713** 🚌 **To Viale Trastevere**

Michelangelo (££)

A hotel with 4-star facilities (including air-conditioning) but at 3-star prices within a stone's throw of the Vatican.

✉ **Via Stazione di S Pietro 14**
☎ **06 622 412/632 359** 🚌 **To Via Stazione di San Pietro**

Perugia (£)

Modest with no frills, but with a friendly multi-lingual staff and most of the 11 rooms have bathrooms. Two steps from the Colosseum.

✉ **Via del Colosseo 7** ☎ **06 679 7200/678 4635** 🚇 **Colosseo**
🚌 **To Via Cavour, Colosseo**

Ponte Sisto (££)

An enormous hotel for the area (130 rooms). It offers all the basic amenities and a terrace in a beautiful part of the historical centre.

✉ **Via dei Pettinari 64**
☎ **06 686 8843/6830 8822**
🚌 **To Via Arenula**

Portoghesi (££)

Tucked away in a lovely side street in one of the prettiest areas. Tastefully furnished, with a roof terrace.

✉ **Via dei Portoghesi 1** ☎ **06 686 4231/687 6976** 🚌 **To Corso del Rinascimento**

San Paolo (£)

Basic but clean and bright on a lovely street, with friendly staff. Twenty rooms (many with own bathroom). Group discounts available.

✉ **Via Panisperna 95** ☎ **06 474 5213/474 5217** 🚇 **Cavour**
🚌 **To Via Cavour**

Sant'Anselmo (££)

A lovely reasonably priced hotel in a villa with garden in the heart of ancient Rome; wheelchair facilities.

✉ **Piazza Sant'Anselmo 2**
☎ **06 578 3214** 🚇 **Circo Massimo** 🚌 **To Via Aventino**

Shangri la' Corsetti (££)

Situated out of the centre beyond EUR. Every amenity including a good restaurant.

✉ **Viale Algeria 141** ☎ **06 591 6441** 🚇 **EUR Fermi**
🚌 **To Palazzo dello Sporto**

Sole al Pantheon (£££)

Next to the Pantheon with some rooms looking over it, this hotel has had some illustrious guests not least Ariosto, one of the greats of Italian literature.

✉ **Piazza della Rotunda 63**
☎ **06 678 0441** 🚌 **To Largo di Torre Argentina**

Self-Catering
Ripa (£££)

One of the main service-apartment options is in Trastevere. All amenities, including a restaurant. Book early, as popular with visiting Italians working in Rome.

✉ **Via Luigi Gianniti** ☎ **06 586 611/581 4550** 🚌 **To Viale Trastevere**

EUR Torrino Residence (££)

A new service-apartment complex near the business district which it serves. Somewhat sterile in the evenings but well-connected to the centre; reasonable prices.

✉ **Via Decima 245** ☎ **06 529 7570** 🚇 **Palasport (then bus)**

Villa Tassoni (££)

This huge turn-of-the-19th-century mansion was built by a general for his family. Now it has been converted into smart studio flats with centralised services. The attractive location of Monte Mario is convenient for the Vatican and the city centre.

✉ **Via delle Medaglie d'Oro 134–8** ☎ **06 355 899/3545 4188** 🚌 **To Vatican**

Youth Hostels

YWCA (£)

The safe women-only hostel near the central station is the perfect option if you are in Rome for early starts and serious sightseeing. There is an evening curfew.

✉ **Via Cesare Balbo 4** ☎ **06 488 0460** 🚇 **Termini** 🚌 **To Via Cavour**

Ostello de la Gioventù Foro Italico (£)

Members of the Youth Hostel Association can stay in this Youth Hostel a little way from the centre. Bed and breakfast, half and full board options.

✉ **Viale delle Olimpiadi 61** ☎ **06 324 2571** 🚌 **To Viale delle Olimpiadi**

Campsites

Parco del Lago (£)

A tranquil campsite set on the edge of Lake Bracciano. All necessary amenities, and popular with Romans who come to get away from it all. Book early. Summer only.

✉ **Strada Provinciale Anguillara Trevignano Km 4,100** ☎ **06 9980 2003** 🚌 **To Anguillara/Trevignano**

Flaminio (£)

A large and reasonably priced campsite within reach of the city, offering cabins among its options. There is a swimming pool. Open March to December.

✉ **Via Flaminia Nuova Km 8,200** ☎ **06 333 2604** 🚌 **Bus or train to Due Ponti**

Castelfusano Country Club (£)

This is actually one of the two campsites near the not-so-clean but long and wide Roman beaches. In Ostia, so Rome is easily reached by public transport. Open all year.

✉ **Piazza di Castelfusano 1** ☎ **06 566 2394** 🚇 **To Castelfusano**

Subiaco

Italia (££)

Open December to March, June to September this hotel with gardens and tennis courts is situated in an off-the-beaten-track area of Lazio in the mountains, yet only 90 minute's drive from Rome. Wonderful local restaurants.

✉ **Via Monte Livata** ☎ **(0774) 826014** 🚌 **Coach to Subiaco**

La Torraccis

Tarquinia Lido (££)

An option which is not-too-distant from Rome and near the Estruscan ruins. Every room has a terrace.

✉ **Viale Mediterraneo 45** ☎ **(0766) 864 375/8642** 🚌 **To Tarquinia**

Tivoli

Delle Terme (££)

This 3-star hotel with its own gardens and restaurant, conveniently placed for the villas of Tivoli, is a fine alternative to staying in the centre, not least because the price goes down by half for the privilege of being in a small attractive countryside town

✉ **Piazza B della Quiete** ☎ **(0774) 371010** 🚌 **To Tivoli**

The Cost of a Star

The Italian star-rating system can make it difficult to know what you are getting, as it is based exclusively on facilities offered. This means, for example, a charmingly furnished atmospheric 2-star affair may cost less than a grotty run-down 3-star business. This is further complicated by a fewer-stars-less-tax situation with some hoteliers happy not to upgrade themselves.

Antiques, Art, Books Toys & Fashion

Where to Find Antiques

If you are looking for antiques (from an old print of Rome to furniture) the most prestigious shops are on Via del Babuino. Another safe and reliable destination is Via Giulia. At the end of May and October, just before and after the blistering heat, Via dei Coronari, which has only antiques, holds its fair. The shops open late, the street is carpeted red and lined with candles. It is a magical atmosphere, perfect for a evening stroll.

Antiques

Arnaboldi
For the more serious collector, this antiques dealer a little out of the centre has everything from porcelain to Russian icons.
- ⊠ Via Gregorio VII 110
- ☎ 06 393 76878 🚍 To Via Gregorio VII

Art Import
A slightly unprepossessing name but a treasure trove if you are after antique silver. They also stock porcelain, an interesting collection of *objéts d'art* and modern Italian Barbini glass vases.
- ⊠ Via del Babuino 150
- ☎ 06 3600 2189 🚇 Spagna
- 🚍 To Piazzale Flaminio

Ramoni
This shop, established in 1930, on another of the important Roman antiques streets, sells everything from furniture to work in silver and bronze. Also an interior design service.
- ⊠ Via Governo Vecchio 76
- ☎ 06 6880 2003 🚍 To Corso Vittorio Emmanuele

Art

Aldo di Castro
Definitely the shop to visit for authentic prints. It stretches far back off the street and is lined with prints of all price ranges. A great selection of framed or unframed Roman scenes.
- ⊠ Via del Babuino 71
- ☎ 06 361 3752 🚇 Spagna
- 🚍 To Piazza San Silvestro, Via del Tritone

Ciambrelli
For a classy canvas or print of pre-20th-century views of

Rome at a reasonable price, this charming and courteous family-run establishment will satisfy your needs.
- ⊠ Via dei Coronari 143
- ☎ 06 6880 1024 🚍 To Corso del Rinascimento

Books

The Corner Bookshop
This small but well-stocked English bookshop in Trastevere offers a good selection of classic and recent fiction and non-fiction, as well as a wide range of books on Italy.
- ⊠ Via del Moro 48 ☎ 06 583 6942 🚍 To Piazza Sonnino

Feltrinelli
The best-stocked bookshop chain in Rome (with a new international outlet near Piazza della Repubblica). Conveniently located branches and easy-to-understand merchandising. Also cards, specialist magazines, posters, videos and CD-Roms.
- ⊠ Via VE Orlando 84/6
- ☎ 06 482 7878
- 🚇 Repubblica 🚍 To Via Nazionale

Libri D'Arte
Out-of-print and rare books not only in Italian, specialising in art books, and posting to anywhere in the world. A little off the beaten track near the Italian TV (RAI) headquarters.
- ⊠ Via Caposile 6 ☎ 06 361 3156 🚍 To Piazza Mazzini

Mel Bookshop
One of the largest, newest bookshops in Rome. 'Mel' has a good English section. It sells everything from kids' books to CDs and even has a

café in the art department.

✉ Via Nationale 254/5
☎ 06 488 5405
🚇 Repubblica
🚌 To Via Nazionale

Touring Viaggi

This bookshop and travel agent of the Touring Club Italiano stocks all you need in terms of maps and guides as well as a small selection of tasteful postcards.

✉ Via del Babuino 20
☎ 06 3609 5801 🚇 Spagna, Flaminio 🚌 To Piazzale Flaminio

Children's Clothes and Toys

La Cicogna

Somewhat pricey but chic high-quality Italian kids' fashion and elegantly practical maternity clothes. Some great bargains if you catch the sales.

✉ Via Cola di Rienzo 268
☎ 06 689 6557 🚌 To Piazza Cavour

Città del Sole

An inspired selection of top-of-the-range educational toys and books for children of all ages. A pretty hands-on, child-friendly approach.

✉ Via della Scrofa 65
☎ 06 687 5404 🚌 To Corso del Rinascimento

Al Sogno

Sogno means dream but this shop could be a parent's nightmare given the prices of the wonderful stock, which sometimes resembles museum pieces. Particularly tempting are the soft toys.

✉ Piazza Navona 53
☎ 06 686 4198 🚌 To Corso del Rinascimento

Invicta

No self-respecting Italian schoolkid can be seen without an 'Invicta' knapsack, so established that it is now officially part of

the Italian language. The new shop includes brand-stretching clothes.

✉ Via del Babuino 27/8
☎ 06 3600 1737 🚇 Spagna
🚌 To Piazzale Flaminio, Piazza San Silvestro

Fashion: designer

Giorgio Armani

The beautifully cut, hand-finished simplicity of the Milanese designer resides in the prestigious Via Condotti. Look for the off-the-peg *Emporio* line which is round the corner on Via del Babuino.

✉ Via Condotti 77 ☎ 06 699 1460 🚇 Spagna 🚌 Via del Corso

Arsenale

Owner Patrizia Pieroni's outlet for her own romantic designs which are an interesting mix between classic and original, and they incorporate the most wonderful velvets, silks, linens and lace.

✉ Via del Governo Vecchio 64
☎ 06 686 1380 🚌 To Corso Vittorio Emanuele

Cenci

High quality, classic and classy. Davide Cenci is synonymous in Rome with low-key tailored elegance and is as refined as an old-style English outfitters. The prices are to match.

✉ Via Campo Marzio 1/7
☎ 06 699 0681 🚌 To Largo di Torre Argentina, Via del Corso

Fendi

There are fur coats, shoes and ready-to-wear clothes, but it is the much-copied signature handbag with the discreet 'F' in the design that is the classic purchase for both Romans and visitors.

✉ Via Borgognona 36–9
☎ 06 679 7641 🚇 Spagna
🚌 To Piazza Augusto Imperatore

Opening and Closing

Shop opening hours are beginning to change with more all-day and Sunday openings and the traditional August shut-down is weakening as Romans begin to take shorter holidays. Generally, however, it is a Monday to Saturday set-up with a break from 1PM to 4PM. Food shops close on Thursday afternoons and others on Monday mornings.

Fashion, Interiors, Jewellery, Leather & Stationery

Prices

Prices in Rome are not low, a state of affairs that is not helped by the preponderance of small shops, which has made for an inefficient retailing system. The tradition is hard to kill. Italian life is public and the local shop, particularly the foodstore, is a place to chat, have things put aside for you, receive discounts and even credit. As a visitor you can expect to be excluded.

VAT Refunds

Non-EU citizens spending more than L.300,000 are entitled to VAT refunds, so be sure to buy from those shops displaying the sticker. You will be furnished with a form to present to customs on leaving Italy along with the *scontrino* (receipt). Do not use or wear the goods first.

Il Discount dell' Alta Moda

Last season's designer clothes, shoes and accessories for men and women at half their original price. A must for bargain hunters.

✉ **Via Gesu' e Maria 16A**
☎ **06 361 3791** 🚍 **To Via del Corso**

Fendissime

Fendi's 'diffusion' label aimed at younger women, has a range of easy to wear, fun clothes, original shoes and classy leather goods, at reasonable prices.

✉ **Via della Fontanella di Borghese 56a** ☎ **06 696661**
🚍 **To Via del Corso, Piazza Augusto Imperatore**

Gucci

Another classic Italian fashion-house offers inimitable wares in a soothing creamy-beige outlet on the most chic street in Rome.

✉ **Via Condotti 8** ☎ **06 678 9340** Ⓜ **Spagna** 🚍 **To Via del Corso**

Missoni

The multi-coloured elegance of the inspired tapestry-like knitwear is almost outrageous. The beach towels offer a taste of the style, if you can not stretch to a sweater.

✉ **Piazza di Spagna 78**
☎ **06 679 2555** Ⓜ **Spagna**
🚍 **To Via del Corso**

Max Mara

The affordable end of designer land, Max Mara offers wonderfully crisp shapes and clean colours in various branches.

✉ **Via Nazionale 28–31**
☎ **06 488 5870** Ⓜ **Repubblica**
🚍 **To Via Nazionale**

Valentino

Rome's own has his boutique on Via Condotti just two steps from the wonderful headquarters in Piazza Mignatelli. The casual wear 'Oliver' is round the corner on Via del Babuino.

✉ **Via Condotti 13** ☎ **06 678 3656** Ⓜ **Spagna** 🚍 **To Via del Corso**

Fashion: 'non-label'

Citoni

Trendy up-to-the-minute fashions for men and women in their twenties and thirties. Lines include the currently highly popular Dolce e Gabbana.

✉ **Via Due Macelli 92–4**
☎ **06 679 5006** Ⓜ **Barberini**
🚍 **To Via del Tritone**

Clark

'Safe' fashions for the twenties upwards. Nothing spectacular but it has good quality at reasonable prices.

✉ **Via Appia Nuova 103 a/b**
☎ **06 049 2552** Ⓜ **San Giovanni, Re di Roma**
🚍 **To Via Appia Nuova**

Gente

One of the best women's clothes shops in Rome, on the city's most popular shopping street. 'Gente' sells lots of wearable styles (including many designer labels). Other branches in the historic centre.

✉ **Via Cola di Renzo 277**
☎ **06 321 1516** 🚍 **To Piazza Cavour**

Lei

For good-quality, fairly pricey but seriously wearable young adult fashions go here. Among others they stock the smart, simple French label Tara. Some shoes and accessories.

✉ Via dei Gubbonari, 103 ☎ 06 687 5432 🚌 To Via Arenula

Interior Design

Azi
An Aladdin's cave of stainless steel, glass and blue and white ceramics for kitchens, bathrooms and the rest of the house. Most of the stock comes from Italy and France.

✉ Via San Francesco a Ripa ☎ 06 588 3303 🚌 To Viale Trastevere

Bagagli
A veritable field-day is to be had in this cobblestoned shop if you want tableware. Villeroy and Boch and the wonderful Alessi designs, which are among the best-quality ranges on offer.

✉ Via di Campo Marzio 42 ☎ 06 687 1406 🚌 To Via del Corso

Cucina
A beautifully merchandised basement shop that stocks top-of-the-range kitchen equipment with impeccable design. Buy your pasta pan here.

✉ Via del Babuino 118-a ☎ 06 679 1275 🚇 Spagna 🚌 To Via del Corso, Piazza San Silvestro

Frette
The queen of household linens. The bed linen and towels, often inspired by classical designs, are quite beautiful, as are the prices unless your trip happens to coincide with the sales.

✉ Via Nazionale 84 ☎ 06 488 2641 🚌 To Via Nazionale

Spazio Sette
By no means cheap but quite easily the best home shop in the centre selling everything

from glassware to hardware, postcards to furniture. The buying philosophy seems to be 'If it is designer...'.

✉ Via dei Barbieri 7 ☎ 06 686 9747 🚌 To Largo di Torre Argentina

Jewellery

Boncompagni
Nicola Boncompagni is a fine shop on a fine street selling a delectable range of antique jewellery.

✉ Via del Babuino 83 ☎ 06 678 3847 🚇 Spagna 🚌 To Via del Corso

Raggi
A fine shop for its wide selection at reasonable prices, with several branches in the city. This branch is on one of the best shopping streets in Rome.

✉ Via Cola di Rienzo 250 ☎ 06 689 6601 🚌 To Piazza Cavour

Vestroni
A small jeweller's which includes in its stock delightful Brugiotti watches reproducing old ceramics on their faces.

✉ Via del Pantheon 42 ☎ 06 687 5813 🚌 To Largo di Torre Argentina

Leather

Bertoletti
With a strong reputation among Romans, this shop is one of the classiest in Rome selling sheepskins, furs and leatherwear.

✉ Via Sistina 42 ☎ 06 678 9625 🚇 Barberini 🚌 To Via del Tritone

Castello D'Auria
A lovely little drawer-lined shop with a small but excellent selection of leather gloves; they also sell hosiery.

✉ Via Due Macelli 55 ☎ 06 679 3364 🚇 Spagna 🚌 To Via del Tritone

Department Stores
Department stores are not the Italian style. If they are yours, the less touristy Piazza Fiume (not far from Via Veneto) is the best bet. Here you will find the larger of the Rinascente (the other is on Via del Corso) with kitchenware, furnishings and a café and, nearby, the old Peroni beer factory has been lovingly converted into Coin.

Shoes, Souvenirs & Markets

Souvenir Shopping

Characteristic Roman souvenirs consist of copies of the main sights or bronze reproductions of Etruscan artefacts, all of which can be found in most tobaccanists at half the price of the stalls near the sights themselves. Ecclesiastical memorabilia is to be had in the shops in and around Borgo Pio, while shops supplying the religious community are on Via dei Cestari near the Pantheon.

Red and Blue

An excellent place to go if you are looking for top-quality leatherwear in the classic styles reflected by its other merchandise, (for example Burberry). Also children's clothes.

✉ **Via due Macelli 57**
☎ **06 679 1933** 🚇 **Spagna**
🚌 **To Via del Tritone**

Accessories

Borsalino

An old-fashioned hat shop which is the most famous in Rome for its classic men's headwear and more changeable women's styles.

✉ **Via IV Novembre 157b**
☎ **06 679 4192** 🚌 **To Piazza Venezia**

Marissa Padovani

The ultimate place to buy swimming costumes – as well as a good range of ready-to-wear, you can have your bikini or one-piece made to measure.

✉ **Via delle Carrozze 81**
☎ **06 679 3946** 🚇 **Spagna**
🚌 **To Via del Corso**

Vision Optika

A massive range of classic and fashion sunglasses, including the latest designer collection (John Paul Gaultier, Police, Sting) which will be altered to fit your face. The shop is also an opticians' studio and can make up prescription lenses.

✉ **Via di S. Claudio 87/a/b**
☎ **06 678 5983** 🚌 **To Piazza San Silvestro**

Stationery

Campo Marzio Penne

Specialises in antique, calligraphic and major-brand pens (and restoration). The new Vatican collection pen is based on designs by Raphael in the Vatican museums.

✉ **Campo Marzio 41** ☎ **06 6880 7877** 🚌 **To Via del Corso**

Pantheon

A gorgeous little shop which sells hand-marbled paper, notebooks and photo albums as well as a great selection of writing paper and cards.

✉ **Via della Rotonda 15**
☎ **06 687 5313** 🚌 **To Largo di Torre Argentina**

Vertecchi

A serious and modern stationery shop selling an excellent selection of pens, writing paper (also by the sheet in a variety of colours). There is a large artist's section.

✉ **Via della Croce 74**
☎ **06 679 0100** 🚇 **Flaminio**
🚌 **To Via del Corso**

Shoes

Dominici

A pristine white-tiled shop in which this Roman designer's original shoes are displayed in neat rows. The prices are good and the styles a bit out of the ordinary without being over the top.

✉ **Via del Corso 14** ☎ **06 361 0591** 🚌 **To Via del Corso**

Impronta

A small shop but with a good collection of young fashion styles. It is on the piazza at the beginning of this atmospheric shopping street.

✉ **Via del Governo Vecchio 1**
☎ **06 689 6947** 🚌 **To Corso Vittorio Emmanuele**

Italya

Tucked away in a side

street near St Lorenzo in Lucina; ladies' own-brand shoes in styles appealing to most age-groups and tastes. There is also a nice selection of bags.

✉ **Via della Torretta 69** ☎ **06 687 1026** 🚊 **To Via del Corso**

Bruno Magli

These incredibly elegant, classic Italian shoes for ladies and gentlemen can be found near the other classic Italian fashion shops.

✉ **Via del Gambero** ☎ **06 679 3802** 🚊 **To Piazza San Silvestro**

Ramirez

Part of a chain and thus competitively priced, this shop can boast a wide selection of shoe styles for both sexes as well as all age groups.

✉ **Via Frattina 85–a** ☎ **06 679 2012** 🚊 **To Via del Corso**

Fausto Santini

The ultimate in modern Roman shoe design, Fausto Santini's styles are original and elegant and you won't find anything quite like them elsewhere.

✉ **Via Frattina 120** ☎ **06 678 4114** 🚇 **Spagna** 🚊 **To Via del Corso**

Souvenirs and Religious Gifts

Gini O Graphics

This sells some great mugs, T-shirts and watches on Roman themes by young designers. There is also fine-art inspired memorabilia, pens and notebooks.

✉ **Via Nazionale 185** ☎ **06 474 6872** 🚊 **To Via Nazionale**

Soprani

One of the many shops around the Vatican dedicated to serious religious artefacts and more commercially minded souvenirs of your trip to the Holy City; images of the Pope and Christ can be printed on almost everything.

✉ **Via del Mascherino 29** ☎ **06 6880 1404** 🚊 **To Piazza del Risorgimento**

Markets

Campo de' Fiori

Probably the loveliest food market in central Rome thanks to the wonderful piazza hosting it. Open every morning except Sundays, the wall of flower-sellers can be found all day.

✉ **Piazza Campo dei Fiori** 🚊 **To Corso Vittorio**

Vittorio Emmanuele

The largest food market in Rome, often criticised for lowering the tone of this splendid piazza with its recently gentrified central garden, is also the cheapest food market. There is a wonderful array of fish and fruit and vegetables.

✉ **Piazza Vittorio Emmanuele** 🚇 **Vittorio** 🚊 **To Piazza Vittorio Emmanuele**

Porta Portese

This market is famous throughout Italy. It takes over the streets in and around Porta Portese every Sunday morning and is jam-packed. You can buy almost everything imaginable from clothes (beware of fake labels) to books and antiques.

✉ **Via Porta Portese** 🚊 **To Viale Trastevere**

Via Sannio

Popular with Romans for new and second-hand clothes. The leather jackets are excellent value and a couple of the shoe stands are good (only if you have the right shoe size). Some real bargains in the piles at the back if you have an eye.

✉ **Via Sannio** 🚇 **San Giovanni** 🚊 **To Via Appia Nuova**

Ancient Sights, Museums & Theme Parks

Christmas
From the beginning of December until Epiphany (6 January) Rome is decorated with delicate street lighting and, on some streets, red carpets. Piazza Navona is taken over by a massive Christmas market selling an exotic range of gaudy sweets, cheap toys and Christmas decorations. In addition many churches have *presepi* (nativity scenes), often with valuable old models placed in realistic Renaissance street scenes.

Ancient Sights
To help get to grips with ancient Rome, the souvenir stands outside the major sights sell little books that show many of the ancient remains as they are now and as they were when they were intact. The gaudy souvenirs on sale here should also appeal to children.

Colosseo (Colosseum)
See the corridors through which lions came on their way to eat Christians. (► 18).

Largo Argentina
Full of serene cats and the remains of a massive public toilet (► 45).

Museo della Civiltà Romana
Models of what ancient Rome was really like (► 48).

Ostia Antica
Well-preserved remains of an ancient Roman seaside town (► 86).

Via Appia Antica
The road ancient Romans travelled on their way to the sea, west to Ostia, east to the other side of Italy (► 62).

Churches

San Clemente
Underneath this pretty mosaic-filled church are secret corridors leading to ancient remains (► 23).

Sant'Ignazio di Loyola
Here you really can see up to heaven by looking at the magnificent *trompe l'oeil* ceiling (► 66).

Santa Maria della Concezione
The macabre crypt is decorated with the bones of defunct monks (► 68).

Santa Maria in Cosmedin
Put your hand into the mouth of truth, which was originally an ancient Roman drain cover and probably represented the sun (► 68).

The Catacombs
Definitely not for the faint-hearted child – these kilometres-long underground passages are lined with the tombs of early Christians (► 38).

Other Sights

Castel Sant'Angelo
This tomb-come-fortress-come-palace has some wonderful *trompe l'oeils* and lots of winding, secret corridors, gloomy guardrooms and good views (► 17).

Galleria Spada
Visit the Galleria in Palazzo Spada particularly for its spectacular three-dimensional *trompe l'oeil*, whose fake perspective will make even the smallest child seem tall (► 56).

Museo delle Cere
The surreality of some of the tableaux may appeal more to adult senses of humour than to children used to Madame Tussaud's, but it is still worth going to see what Leonardo and his contemporaries might have looked like.
✉ Piazza dei Santi Apostoli 67 ☎ 06 679 6482 ◉ Apr–Sept, 9–9. Oct–Mar, 9–8 🚌 To Piazza Venezia

Museo del Folklore e dei Poeti Romaneschi

As well as paintings of what Rome looked like when all these artists were strolling around, there are some amusing waxworks of Roman and rustic life in the 18th century (➤ 48).

Outdoor: Parks and Shows

Aquafelix

A water park with an exotic range of themed rides and slides involving getting wet and screaming – most children under five may find it a little too much. There are also shops, a bar and a self-service restaurant.

✉ **Autostrada Roma–Civitavecchia at the Civitavecchia Nord Exit** ☎ **(0766) 32221** ⏰ **Jun–Sep, 10–6 daily**

Aquapiper

An outdoor swimming pool complex with a children's pool complete with a slide, an adult/older children's pool with a wave machine and its own more exciting (or terrifying, depending on your point of view) slide. There are also ponies and camels, a picnic area, a bar and a games room.

✉ **Via Maremmana Inferiore Km 29, Guidonia** ☎ **(0774) 326 538** ⏰ **First week Jun to first week Sep, Mon–Fri 9–6:30, Sat & Sun 9–7** 🚌 **From Ponte Mammolo to Palombara**

Bioparco

Rome's zoo underwent a transformation in the late 1990s to re-emerge as a champion of environmental awareness. In place of the old museum mentality, visitors are encouraged to learn more about the natural habitats of the animals and to play an active part in their conservation.

✉ **Piazzale del Giardino Zoologico, Villa Borghese** ☎ **06 360 8211** ⏰ **8:30–6** 🚌 **To Piazza Ungheria**

Piazza Navona

There is always plenty to see here; you can pose for a portrait or caricature, buy a helium-filled balloon or eat ice-cream. There is Bernini's wonderful fountain to set your imagination flying (➤ 21).

Puppet Shows

Although these are in Italian (and a fairly dialectic Italian at that) they are more or less comprehensible to anybody, being variations on the traditional 'Punch and Judy' theme. There are also fairground-type stalls and a roundabout nearby.

✉ **Piazza Garibaldi** ⏰ **Summer weekday eve, all year Sun AM** 🚌 **To Gianicolo** 🎩 **A hat is passed around**

Luna Park

This 30-year-old funfair is the nearest that Rome gets to a theme park. Most of its attractions are fairly traditional – a hall of mirrors, a ferris wheel, roller-coasters and merry-go-rounds – but recent additions include some more ambitious contraptions and stage-sets based on American theme-park rides.

✉ **Via delle Tre Fontane** ☎ **592 5933** ⏰ **Jun–Sep, Mon–Fri 5–12, Sat 3–1, Sun 3–12; Sept–Jun, Mon, Wed–Fri 3–7, Sat 3–1, Sun 10–1, 3–10** 🚇 **Magliana** 🚌 **To Via delle Tre Fontane**

Carnevale

Carnevale takes place the week before Shrove Tuesday and children dress up as cartoon or historical characters, animals and so on to walk through the streets with their parents, letting off fire crackers and throwing confetti.

Cinema, Theatre, Music & Opera

Hollywood on the Tiber

Rome has had an active film industry since 1937 when Mussolini opened the studios at Cinecittà. The heyday of 'Hollywood on the Tiber' was in the 1950s and 1960s when many American producers and directors came here to make films such as *Ben Hur*, *Cleopatra* and, of course, the famous spaghetti westerns. Things have quietened down a bit since then but the studios are still used by Italian film and TV makers and guided tours are sometimes arranged (phone to check).

✉ Via Tuscolana 1055
☎ 06 722931
🚇 Cinecittà 🚌 502, 503, 504, 506, 551, 558, 561

Cinema

Italy is proud of its high standard of dubbing and most foreign films are dubbed into Italian. Cinema screenings are usually at 4:30, 6:30, 8:30 and 10:30. In the summer (June to September), there are several open-air cinemas, showing mainly classics or the previous season's most successful releases.

L'Alcazar

Recent releases in Trastevere. Films shown in English or with English sub-titles on Mondays.

✉ Via Cardinal Merry del Val 14 ☎ 06 588 0099
🚌 To Viale Trastevere, Piazza Sonnino

Majestic

Mainstream cinema near Piazza Venezia. Shows films in English on Mondays.

✉ Via Santi Apostoli 20
☎ 06 679 4908 🚌 To Piazza Venezia

Nuovo Sacher

This cinema belongs to film-maker Nanni Moretti (of *Caro Diario* fame) and is named after his favourite cake. It shows slightly offbeat new releases (which appeal to the proprietor) and screens them in original language (which can be anything) on Mondays and Tuesdays. There is an outdoor arena where films are shown during the summer.

✉ Largo Ascianghi 1
☎ 06 581 8116 🚌 To Viale Trastevere

Pasquino

The new management recently overhauled 'Pasquino', the first English language cinema in Rome.

The 2 cinemas show English-language films only (usually with Italian sub-titles).

✉ Vicolo del Piede 19
☎ 06 580 3622 🚌 To Viale Trastevere, Piazza Sonnino

Warner Village Moderno

Five large screens in this utra-modern complex – new releases in English every Thursday. Great sound and comfy seats.

✉ Piazza della Repubblica 45/6 ☎ 06 477791
🚇 Repubblica 🚌 40, 60, 64, 170 to Piazza della Repubblica

Outdoor Cinema

Massenzio

The main summer cinema venue, which has no official fixed abode but has recently been on the park opposite the entrance to the Palatino. Three films a night, ranging from the previous season's releases to erudite festivals by international stars of the film-making world. There is a lively jazz and music festival going on at the same time.

✉ Parco del Celio, entrance on Via di San Gregorio.

Piazza Vittorio

Weekly original-language (usually English) films in the pristine Piazza Vittorio gardens. Also holds other events, including activities for children from Jul–Sep.

✉ Piazza Vittorio ☎ 06 445 1208/291

Theatre and Dance

Agorà

This theatre hosts visiting theatre companies from the rest of Europe. Plays in

Italian, English, French, Spanish and so on depending on who is here.

✉ Via della Penitenza 33
☎ 06 687 4167 🚍 To Lungotevere Farnesina

dell'Angelo

A fairly recent-comer to the theatre scene. Productions include some avant-garde Italian and foreign companies. There is also an interesting programme of contemporary and jazz music.

✉ Via Simon de San Bon 17
☎ 06 3600 2640
Ⓜ Ottaviano 🚍 To Largo Trionfale

Argentina

A beautiful, restored 19th-century gem which occasionally hosts TV spectaculars. Home to the Rome Theatre Company, who do good (if slightly traditional) productions of ancient and modern classics.

✉ Largo di Torre Argentina 52
☎ 06 6880 4601 🚍 To Largo di Torre Argentina

Colosseo

One of the best venues for seeing works by young Italian directors and playwrights.

✉ Via Capo d'Africa 5a
☎ 06 700 4932 Ⓜ Colosseo
🚍 81, 85

Olimpico

A vast barn of a place where international dance and musical productions are staged. It is also where the Rome Philharmonic Orchestra holds its concerts.

✉ Piazza Gentile da Fabriano 17 ☎ 06 323 4890 🚍 To Piazza Mancini

Sistina

This is the place to come for musicals, either homegrown or Italianised versions of London and New York hits.

✉ Via Sistina 129 ☎ 06 482 6841 Ⓜ Barberini 🚍 To Piazza Barberini

Valle

One of two venues for the National Italian Theatre company. Excellent productions of modern classics such as Pirandello, Beckett and Pinter.

✉ Via del Teatro Valle 23a
☎ 06 6880 3794 🚍 To Corso Vittorio Emanuele

Vascello

As well as hosting some of the most interesting theatre companies in Italy, this is a venue for ballet, contemporary and ethnic dance.

✉ Via Giacinto Carini 72
☎ 06 588 1021 🚍 41, 44, 75

Music: Classical and Opera

Auditorio di Santa Cecilia

The Accademia has one of Rome's best chamber and symphony orchestras, who perform here, often under the baton of top-class visiting conductors.

✉ Via della Conciliazione 4
☎ 06 6880 1844 🚍 To Piazza del Risorgimento

Teatro Olimpico

Where the Filarmonica di Roma, and its visiting performers and ensembles, perform. (► Theatre and Dance, above).

Teatro dell'Opera

The winter season of the Rome opera and ballet company takes place here. In summer performances are staged in the Piazza di Siena, in the Villa Borghese.

✉ Via Firenze 72 ☎ 06 481601 Ⓜ Termini 🚍 To Termini,

Music: Jazz, Rock

Alexanderplatz

The place for jazz in Rome. A restaurant and cocktail bar.

✉ Via Ostia 9 ☎ 06 3974 2171 Ⓜ Ottaviano
🚍 To Largo Trionfale

Ancient Theatre

For an authentic ancient Roman theatre experience head down to the well-preserved ancient Roman theatre at Ostia Antica (► 86) in July and August when the Teatro Romano produces classical Roman and Greek plays. Alternatively, at the Vatican end of the Gianicolo (► 43) lies the little amphitheatre of Tasso's Oak, where ancient and less ancient classics are performed against the backdrop of wonderful views of the city.

Anfiteatro della Quercia del Tasso

✉ Passeggiata del Gianicolo ☎ (07) 575 0827 🕐 Jul–Sep 🚍 41, 44 Teatro Romano di Ostia Antica ✉ Ostia Antica ☎ 06 687 7390 🕐 Jul–Aug 🚆 Train to Ostia Antica

Music, Clubs, Bars & Sport

Outdoor Music

During the summer there are plenty of outdoor classical musical events, including a series of Sunday morning concerts given by the orchestras of various branches of the armed forces on the Pincio. For a combination of world-class performers and a staggeringly beautiful setting, head to Villa Giulia (► 78) which is where the Accademia di Santa Cecilia hosts its summer season. Other top-quality performers can be heard under the remains of Teatro di Marcello (► 74).

Teatro di Marcello

✉ Via del Teatro di Marcello 44
☎ Information about the concerts: 06 481 4800
🕐 Jun–Oct
🚊 To Via del Teatro di Marcello

Terme di Caracalla

✉ Via della Terme di Caracalla 52
☎ Information about the concerts: 06 575 8626
🕐 Jun–Oct
🚌 160, 613, 628, 714
♿ Few

Villa Giulia

✉ Piazzale di Villa Giulia 9
☎ Information about the concerts: 06 678 6428
🕐 Jul 🚌 19, 19b, 30, 30b, 225, 926

Alpheus

Three separate areas: one catering for jazz, one for rock and the other for dancing to records.
✉ Via del Commercio 36
☎ 06 574 7826 🚇 Piramide
🚊 To Via Ostiense

Big Mama

Sub-titled 'the home of the blues in Rome', Big Mama has an interesting programme of live music performed by Italian and international musicians, including the occasional legend.
✉ Vicolo San Francesco a Ripa 18 ☎ 06 581 2551
🚊 To Viale Trastevere

Bossanova

One of the Latin-American venues, with a mixture of live and recorded music and dancing.
✉ Via degli Orti di Trastevere 43 ☎ 06 581 6121
🚊 To Viale Trastevere

Circolo degli Artisti

Some of the most recent big names from the international music scene play here. It is also a good place for dancing and organises nights of 1960s, African and so on music, as well as hosting visiting DJs from the rest of Europe.
✉ Via Lamarmora 28
☎ 06 446 4968

Il Locale

Small, friendly venue near Piazza Navona with mainly Italian live music.
✉ Vicolo del Fico 3
☎ 06 687 9075 🚊 To Corso Vittorio Emanuele

Palladium

A converted cinema that now hosts largeish-scale rock concerts as well as specialised dance and other music events.
✉ Piazza Bartolomeo Romano 8 ☎ 06 511 0203
🚇 Garbetella 🚊 92, 770

Saint Louis Music City

Another fun, jazz venue with strongly American-themed decor.
✉ Via del Cardello 13a
☎ 06 474 5076 🚇 Cavour
🚊 To Via Cavour, Via dei Fori Imperiali

Stadio Olimpico

A sports stadium that hosts the very biggest Italian and foreign rock names to come to Rome.
✉ Via dei Gladiatori ☎ 06 323 7333 🚊 To Lungotevere Maresciallo Cadorna

Stazione Ouagadougou

A new-comer offering live and recorded African music in a spectacularly furnished venue.
✉ Via della Lungaretta 75
☎ 06 581 2510 🚊 To Viale Trastevere

Nightclubs and Bars

Alibi

A hetero-friendly gay club in the throbbing Testaccio area.
✉ Via di Monte Testaccio 44
☎ 06 574 3448 🚇 Piramide
🚊 To Via Marmorata

Alien

Vast mainstream disco with *cubistes* (scantily clad girls, and a few boys, who dance on top of columns for those who cannot be bothered to move themselves).
✉ Via Velletri 13 ☎ 06 841 2212 🚊 To Piazza Fiume

Caffè Latina

One of the earliest of the Testaccio clubs to open. In spite of its name you're as likely to hear jazz, blues or rock music as you are Latin American.

✉ **Via di Monte Testaccio 96**
☎ **06 574 4020** 🚇 **Piramide**
🚌 **To Via Marmarata**

Gilda

The establishment place to bop (or watch others), frequented by, among others, right-wing politicians and TV personalities.

✉ **Via Mario de' Fiori 97**
☎ **06 679 7396** 🚌 **To Piazza San Silvestro**

Jonathan's Angels

A beautifully decorated cocktail bar, covered with the paintings of its biker owner, Jonathan.

✉ **Via della Fossa 16**
☎ **06 689 3426** 🚌 **To Corso del Rinascimento, Corso Vittorio Emanuele**

Piper

The place of the Dolce Vita 1960s; now a non-threatening club for those who do not do much clubbing.

✉ **Via Tagliamento 9**
☎ **06 855 5398** 🚌 **56, 57, 319**

La Vineria

In summer, the clients of this little wine bar spill out into Campo de' Fiori. Popular with trendy foreigners.

✉ **Campo de' Fiori 15**
☎ **06 6880 3268** 🚌 **To Corso Vittorio Emanuele**

Sport

ATAC Dopolavoro

The city bus company employees' social club rents out its tennis courts to the public.

✉ **Lungotevere Thaon di Revel 11–13** ☎ **06 702 2637**
🕐 **Mon–Sat 8AM–11PM; Sun 8–8; book the day before**
🚌 **To Piazza Mancini**

Cavalieri Hilton

At a price you can enjoy the luxury of the Hilton's outdoor swimming pool.

✉ **Via Cadlolo 101**
☎ **06 35091** 🕐 **May–Sept: 9–7** 🚌 **907, 913, 991, 999**

Foro Italico

The annual International Tennis Tournament, the Italian Open, is held here for two weeks in mid-May.

✉ **Viale dei Gladiatori 31**
☎ **Information: 06 321 9064**
🚌 **Lungotevere Maresciallo Cadorna**

Ippodromo delle Campanelle

This is Rome's horse-racing track. Races are held from September to June.

✉ **Via Appia Nuova 1255**
☎ **06 718 8750** 🚌 **663, 664**

Piazza Siena

The elegant horse show takes place in the little arena in Villa Borghese every May.

✉ **Villa Borghese**
☎ **Information: 06 3974 0789**
🚌 **To Piazzale Flaminio**

Piscina delle Rose

Aptly named public swimming pool where you can hire sun-beds and umbrellas. There is also a bar.

✉ **Viale America 20** ☎ **06 592 6717** 🚇 **EUR Palasport**
🚌 **To Piazzale dello Sport**

Roman Sport Centre

Daily membership allows you access to the gyms of one of Rome's most exclusive sports and fitness clubs.

✉ **The car park underneath Villa Borghese** ☎ **06 320 1667**
🕐 **Mon–Sat 9AM–10PM, Sun 9–3** 🚇 **Spagna** 🚌 **To Via Veneto**

Stadio Olimpico

Both the football teams, AS Roma and Lazio play here.

✉ **Via dei Gladiatori** ☎ **06 3685 7520** 🚌 **To Lungotevere Maresciallo Cadorna**

Swim, Sun, Sand

It may not be the best way to escape the crowds, but a day at the beach is a good break from sightseeing, especially during the week. Entrepreneurs sometimes limit beach access to those renting sunbeds and parasols, but this is not always the case. Bars and restaurants offer lunch. The nearest beaches are at Ostia (metro from Magliana), Fregene and Torvaianica. Further afield are Sperlonga (► 87) to the south and Santa Marinella to the north.

What's On When

Villaggio Globale
The old abattoir in the centre of Testaccio has been taken over and converted into the Villaggio Globale, a cultural centre for exhibitions, concerts and dance events. In the summer the vast central courtyard (originally used for herding animals) is given over to an excellent festival of world music with side stalls and an interesting range of international refreshment stands.

✉ Lungotevere Testaccio
☎ 06 5730 0329 🚌 27, 92

January
New Year's Day: public holiday.
6 Jan: Epiphany, public holiday. Traditionally the *befana* (witch) leaves presents for children.

February
Week leading up to Shrove Tuesday: *Carnevale* (➤ 111), streets full of adults and children in fancy dress. Shrove Tuesday: *Martedi grasso* celebrations (in costume) in Piazza Navona (➤ 21) and elsewhere.

March/April
9 Mar: cars, buses and taxis blessed at the church of San Francesca Romana (the patron saint of motorists) in the Forum (➤ 22).
Mid-Mar onwards: Spanish Steps (➤ 60) decorated with huge azalea plants.
Good Friday: Pope leads the ceremony of the Stations of the Cross at the Colosseo (Colosseum) (➤ 18).
Easter Sunday: papal address at St Peter's.
Easter Monday: public holiday.
21 Apr: Rome's birthday, bands and orchestras perform at Campidoglio, (➤ 16) Piazza di Spagna (➤ 60) and elsewhere.
25 Apr: Liberation Day, public holiday to commemorate the Allies' liberation of Rome from the Nazis in 1944.

May
1 May: Labour Day, public holiday, no public transport, huge free rock concert in Piazza di San Giovanni in Laterano.
Early May: horse show at Piazza di Siena.

Mid-May to Oct: rose garden above Circo Massimo (➤ 39) open to the public.
Mid-May: International Tennis Tournament (➤ 115).

June/July
Mid-Jun to Sep: outdoor concerts, cinemas, fairs and other arts events all over the city.
End-Jun to mid-Sep: *Estate Romana*. The ever expanding festival offering open-air cinema, music, theatre and arts events around the city.
Mid to late Jul: *Festa de Noantri*, stalls, concerts and other cultural events in Trastevere.

August
15 Aug: *Ferragosto*, public holiday, lots of shops, restaurants, bars and businesses close for a week or more.

October
Early Oct: wine festivals in towns near Rome, and a small one in Trastevere.

November
1 Nov: All Saints, public holiday.
Mid-Nov: the new season's *vini novelli* ready for drinking.

December
Beginning Dec to 6 Jan: Christmas fair in Piazza Navona (➤ 21, 110).
8 Dec: Immaculate Conception, public holiday.
Christmas time: *presepi* (nativity scenes) on show in churches and main piazzas.
25 Dec: Christmas Day, public holiday, papal address in St Peter's Square.
31 Dec: New Year's Eve celebrations, fireworks and concerts in Piazza del Popolo and elsewhere in the city.

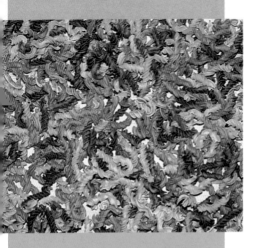

Practical
Matters

Above: *fusilli pasta*
Below: *Roman police*

TIME DIFFERENCES

GMT 12 noon	Rome 1PM →	Germany 1PM →	USA (NY) 7AM ←	Netherlands 1PM →	Spain 1PM →

BEFORE YOU GO

WHAT YOU NEED

- ● Required
- ○ Suggested
- ▲ Not required

	UK	Germany	USA	Netherlands	Spain
Passport/National Identity Card	●	●	●	●	●
Visa	▲	▲	▲	▲	▲
Onward or Return Ticket	▲	▲	▲	▲	▲
Health Inoculations	▲	▲	▲	▲	▲
Health Documentation (reciprocal agreement document) (► 123, Health)	●	●	▲	●	●
Travel Insurance	○	○	○	○	○
Driving Licence (national)	●	●	●	●	●
Car Insurance Certificate (if own car)	○	○	○	○	○
Car Registration Document (if own car)	●	●	●	●	●

WHEN TO GO

Rome

■ High season
☐ Low season

7°C	8°C	11°C	14°C	18°C	23°C	26°C	25°C	22°C	18°C	13°C	9°C
JAN	FEB	MAR	APR	MAY	JUN	JUL	AUG	SEP	OCT	NOV	DEC

☁ Wet   ☁ Cloud   ☀ Sun

TOURIST OFFICES

In the UK
Italian State Tourist Board
1 Princes Street
London W1R 8AY
☎ 020 7408 1254
Fax: 020 7493 6695

In the USA
Italian State Tourist Board
630 Fifth Avenue
Suite 1565
New York NY 10111
☎ 212/245 4822
Fax: 212/586 9242

Italian State Tourist Board
12400 Wilshire Boulevard
Suite 550
Los Angeles, CA 90025
☎ 310/820 1959
Fax: 310/820 6357

POLICE 113   CARABINIERI 112

FIRE 115

ANY EMERGENCY (including AMBULANCE) 113

ROAD ASSISTANCE (ACI) 116

WHEN YOU ARE THERE

ARRIVING

There are direct flights from Europe and North America. Alitalia (☎ 06 65631) is the national airline. Rome has two airports: Leonardo da Vinci, also known as Fiumicino (☎ 06 65951), is the larger and handles scheduled flights, while Ciampino (☎ 06 794941) caters mostly for charter flights.

Leonardo da Vinci (Fiumicino) Airport
Kilometres to city centre

26 kilometres

Journey times	
🚌	30 or 45 minutes
🚆	50 minutes
🚗	40 minutes

Ciampino Airport
Kilometres to city centre

13 kilometres

Journey times	
🚌	20 minutes after bus
🚆	15 minutes (to train)
🚗	30 minutes

MONEY

The monetary unit of Italy is the lira (plural lire), abbreviated to Lit or L. The denominations are: coins of 50, 100, 200, 500 and 1,000 lire and notes of 1,000, 2,000, 5,000, 10,000, 50,000, 100,000 and 500,000 lire. In 1999 the lira became a denomination of the euro. Lira notes and coins continue to be legal tender during a transitional period. Euro bank notes and coins are due to be introduced by January 2002.

TIME

Italy is one hour ahead of Greenwich Mean Time (GMT+1), but from late March, when clocks are put forward one hour, to late September, Italian Summer Time (GMT+2) operates.

CUSTOMS

**YES
From another EU country for personal use (guidelines):**
800 cigarettes, 200 cigars,
1 kilogram of tobacco
10 litres of spirits (over 22%)
20 litres of aperitifs
90 litres of wine, of which 60 litres can be sparkling wine
110 litres of beer

From a non-EU country for your personal use, the allowances are:
200 cigarettes OR
50 cigars OR 20 grams of tobacco
1 litre of spirits (over 22%)
2 litres of intermediary products (e.g. sherry) and sparkling wine
2 litres of still wine
50 grams of perfume
0.25 litres of eau de toilette
The value limit for goods is 175 euros

Travellers under 17 years of age are not entitled to the tobacco and alcohol allowances

NO
Drugs, firearms, ammunition, offensive weapons, obscene material, unlicensed animals.

119

EMBASSIES

UK	**Germany**	**USA**	**Netherlands**	**Spain**
482 5441	884741	46741	322 1141	580 0144

WHEN YOU ARE THERE

TOURIST OFFICES

Ente Provinciale Tourismo (Rome Provincial Tourist Board)

Offices:
- Via Parigi 5
  ☎ 06 4889 9253
  🕐 Mon–Sat 8:15–7

- Leonardo da Vinci (Fiumicino) Airport
  ☎ 06 6595 6074
  🕐 Mon–Sat 8:15–7

- Stazione Termini (Main Railway Station)
  ☎ 06 487 1270
  🕐 daily 8:15–7.15

Info-Tourism Kiosks:
  🕐 Tue–Sat 10–6; Sun 10–1

- Largo Carlo Goldoni, Via del Corso
  ☎ 06 6813 6061

- Via Nazionale
  ☎ 06 4782 4525

- Fori Imperiali
  Piazza del Tempio della
  Pace ☎ 06 6902 4307

- Piazza Navona
  Piazza Cinque Lune
  ☎ 06 6880 9240

- Santa Maria Maggiore
  Via dell'Olmata
  ☎ 06 4788 0294

NATIONAL HOLIDAYS

J	F	M	A	M	J	J	A	S	O	N	D
2		1	2	1			1			1	3

1 Jan	New Year's Day
6 Jan	Epiphany
Mar/Apr	Easter Monday
25 Apr	Liberation Day, 1945
1 May	Labour Day
15 Aug	Assumption of the Virgin
1 Nov	All Saints' Day
8 Dec	Immaculate Conception
25 Dec	Christmas Day
26 Dec	St Stephen's Day

Banks, businesses and most shops and museums close on these days. Rome celebrates its patron saint (St Peter) on 29 June, but generally most places remain open.

OPENING HOURS

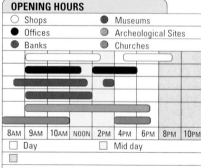

○ Shops	● Museums
● Offices	● Archeological Sites
● Banks	● Churches

☐ Day   ☐ Mid day

In addition to the times in the chart, department stores, some supermarkets, plus shops in tourist areas may not close lunchtime, and sometimes remain open until later in the evening. Some shops shut Monday morning and in summer may close Saturday afternoon. Most shops close Sunday. Some banks open until 2PM and do not reopen in the afternoon. All are closed weekends.
Some museums also open in the afternoon (usually 5–8PM). Many museums close early on Sunday (around 1PM) and most are closed Mondays.

DRIVE ON THE
RIGHT

TOILETS
CHARGE

PUBLIC TRANSPORT

Internal Flights Services throughout the country are provided by Alitalia – the national airline (☎ 06 65641), and its associated companies ATI (☎ (020) 8709 1111) and Avianova (☎ 06 655 1617). The flight time to Rome from Milan is 65 minutes; from Florence 75 minutes; and from Naples 45 minutes.

Trains Italian State Railways (Ferrovie dello Stato, or FS) provide an efficient service. Almost all long-distance trains to Rome arrive and depart from Stazione Termini (some fast trains use Stazione Roma Tiburtina). Stazione Termini is shut from midnight to 5AM, then trains stop at other city stations. Timetable information ☎ 147 888088

Long Distance Buses There is no national bus company but COTRAL (☎ 06 591 5551) has the major presence in Rome, serving the Lazio region. Buses depart from numerous points throughout the city, depending on their destinations. For details of who goes where, ask at the nearest tourist information office.

Urban Transport Buses (yellow), plus in the outer districts trams, are the best way to get around, though the complexity of the routes can be daunting. Bus or tram stops (*fermata*) have yellow signs. You must have a ticket before boarding at the rear (*salita*) and your ticket stamped in the machine there. Exit through the middle door (*uscita*). The underground (*Metropolitana* or *Metrò*) – entrances: white 'M' on red – has only two lines: *Linea A* (red) runs from Battistini to Anagnina in the southeast. *Linea B* (blue) runs from Rebibbia in the northeast to EUR in the southwest. Tickets from machines at stations.

CAR RENTAL

Car hire (*autonoleggio*) is at airports, the main railway station, and city offices, but driving in Rome is not recommended and not cheap. Small local firms offer the best rates but cars can only be booked locally. Air or train travellers can benefit from inclusive deals.

TAXIS

Taxis can be hailed on the street, found at a taxi rank (stations and major piazze), or phoned 06 3570, 3875, 4994 or 8433). There is an initial charge and a rate for each kilometre. Traffic can mean stiff meter increases and there are Sunday and late-night supplements.

DRIVING

Speed limits on motorways (*autostrade*), which have tolls: **130kph**

Speed limits on main roads: **110kph**; secondary roads: **90kph**

Speed limits on urban roads: **50kph**

Must be worn in front seats at all times and in rear seats where fitted.

Random breath-testing is frequent. Limit: 80mg per 100ml blood.

Petrol (*benzina*) is more expensive in Italy than in Britain and most other European countries. All except small garages in out-of-the-way places sell unleaded petrol (*senza piombo*). Outside urban areas filling stations open 7AM to 12:30PM and 3 to 7:30PM. Motorway service stations are open 24 hours. Credit cards are rarely accepted.

In the event of a breakdown, ring 116, giving your registration number and type of car and the nearest ACI (Automobile Club d'Italia) office will be informed to assist you. You will be towed to the nearest ACI garage. This service is free to foreign-registered vehicles or cars rented from Rome or Milan airports (you will need to produce your passport!)

PERSONAL SAFETY

In Rome, petty theft (bag and neck-chain snatching, pick-pocketing and car break-ins) is the main problem. The police (*polizia*) to whom thefts should be reported wear light-blue trousers and dark-blue jackets. Some precautions:
- Carry shoulder bags not *on* your shoulder but slung *across* your body.
- Scooter-borne bag-snatchers can be foiled if you keep on the *inside* of the pavement.
- Do not put anything down on a café or restaurant table.
- Lock car doors and never keep valuables in your car.

Police assistance:
☎ **113** from any call box

TELEPHONES

Almost every bar in Italy has a telephone, plus many in public places. They take 100, 200 or 500 Lire coins and more often phone-cards (*Schede telefoniche*) for 5,000 and 10,000 Lire. Phonecards are available from SIP (state telephone company) offices, tobac-conists, stations and other public places.

International Dialling Codes	
From Rome to:	
UK:	**00 44**
Germany:	**00 49**
USA:	**00 1**
Netherlands:	**00 31**
Spain:	**00 34**

POST

Post Offices
The city's main post office is on Piazza San Silvestro.
🕒 8.25AM–7.40PM (8.20–11.50AM Sat). Closed: Sun
☎ 160
Vatican City has its own postal system, with a post office in St Peter's Square.
🕒 8.30AM–7PM (6PM Sat) Closed: Sun ☎ 69 82

ELECTRICITY

The power supply is: 220 volts (in parts of Rome: 125 volts).

Type of socket: Round two- or three-hole sockets takings plugs of two round pins, or sometimes three pins in a vertical row. British visitors should bring an adaptor; US visitors a voltage transformer.

TIPS/GRATUITIES

Yes ✓ No ✗		
Hotels (if service not included)	✓	(10–15%)
Restaurants (if service not included)	✓	(10–15%)
Cafés/bars	✓	(L200)
Taxis	✓	(15%)
Porters	✓	(L2,000)
Chambermaids	✓	(L3,000/wkly)
Cinema/theatre usherettes	✓	(L1,000)
Hairdressers	✓	(L3,000)
Cloakroom attendants	✓	(L1,000)
Toilets	✓	(L100 min)

PHOTOGRAPHY

Light: The light in Rome is good: neither the glare of the south nor the hazier light of the north of the country.

Where you can photograph: Most museums and certain churches will not allow you to photograph inside; check first.

Film and developing: A roll of film is called a *pellicola*, but 'film' should get you understood. Film and developing are much more expensive in Italy than in the UK or USA.

HEALTH

Insurance
Nationals of EU and certain other countries receive reduced cost medical (including hospital) treatment and pay a percentage of prescribed medicines. You need a qualifying document (Form E111 for Britons). Private medical insurance is still advised.

Dental Services
Nationals of EU and certain other countries can obtain dental treatment at a reduced cost at dentists within the Italian health service. A qualifying document (Form E111 for Britons) is needed. Private medical insurance is still advised.

Sun Advice
In summer, particularly in July and August, it can get oppressively hot and humid in the city. If 'doing the sights' cover up or apply a sunscreen (or dive into the shade of a museum), plus take in plenty of fluids.

Drugs
A pharmacy (*farmacia*), recognised by a green cross sign, will possess highly trained staff able to offer medical advice on minor ailments and provide a wide range of prescribed and non-prescribed medicines and drugs.

Safe Water
Rome is famed for its drinking water, which is generally safe, even from outdoor fountains (unless you see a sign saying *acqua non potabile*). However, Romans prefer the taste of bottled mineral

CONCESSIONS

Students/Youths Holders of an International Student Identity Card (ISIC), and for those under 26 an International Youth Card (IYC) – available from student organisations – can take advantage of discounts on transport, accommodation, museum entrance fees, car hire and in restaurants. Nationals (under 18) of EU and certain other countries receive free admission to state museums.

Senior Citizens Citizens aged over 60 of EU and a number of other countries with which Italy has a reciprocal arrangement (not including the USA) may gain free admission to communal and state museums and receive discounts at other museums and on public transport on production of their passport.

CLOTHING SIZES

Italy	UK	Rest of Europe		
46	36	46	36	Suits
48	38	48	38	
50	40	50	40	
52	42	52	42	
54	44	54	44	
56	46	56	46	
41	7	41	8	Shoes
42	7.5	42	8.5	
43	8.5	43	9.5	
44	9.5	44	10.5	
45	10.5	45	11.5	
46	11	46	12	
37	14.5	37	14.5	Shirts
38	15	38	15	
39/40	15.5	39/40	15.5	
41	16	41	16	
42	16.5	42	16.5	
43	17	43	17	
38	8	34	6	Dresses
40	10	36	8	
42	12	38	10	
44	14	40	12	
46	16	42	14	
48	18	44	16	
38	4.5	38	6	Shoes
38	5	38	6.5	
39	5.5	39	7	
39	6	39	7.5	
40	6.5	40	8	
41	7	41	8.5	

WHEN DEPARTING

- Contact the airport or airline on the day prior to leaving to ensure the flight details are unchanged.
- The airport departure tax, payable when you leave Italy, is included in the cost of the airline ticket.
- Check the duty-free limits of the country you are travelling to before departure.

LANGUAGE

Italian is the native language but Romans speak a dialect with its own particular stresses, intonations and vocabulary, of which they are fiercely proud. Many Romans speak English but you will be better received if you at least attempt to communicate in Italian. Italian words are pronounced phonetically. Every vowel and consonant (except 'h') is sounded. The accent usually (but not always) falls on the penultimate syllable. Below is a list of a few words that may be helpful. More extensive coverage can be found in the AA's *Essential Italian Phrase Book* which lists over 2,000 phrases and 2,000 words.

hotel	*albergo*	breakfast	*prima colazione*
room	*camera*	toilet	*toilette*
..single/double	*....singola/doppia*	bath	*bagno*
..one/two nights	*per una/due notte/i*	shower	*doccia*
		balcony	*balcone*
..one/two people	*....per una/due persona/e*	reception	*reception*
		key	*chiave*
reservation	*prenotazione*	room service	*servizio da camera*
rate	*tariffa*	chambermaid	*cameriera*

bank	*banco*	bank note	*banconota*
exchange office	*cambio*	coin	*moneta*
post office	*posta*	credit card	*carta di credito*
cashier	*cassiere/a*	traveller's cheque	*assegno turistico*
foreign exchange	*cambio con l'estero*	cheque book	*libretto degli assegni*
foreign currency	*valuta estera*		
pound sterling	*sterlina*	exchange rate	*tasso di cambio*
American dollar	*dollaro*	commission charge	*commissione*

restaurant	*ristorante*	starter	*il primo*
café	*caffè*	main course	*il secondo*
table	*tavolo*	dish of the day	*piatto del giorno*
menu	*menù/carta*	dessert	*dolci*
set menu	*menù turistico*	drink	*bevanda*
wine list	*lista dei vini*	waiter	*cameriere*
lunch	*pranzo/colazione*	waitress	*cameriera*
dinner	*cena*	the bill	*conto*

aeroplane	*aeroplano*	..single/return	*....andata sola/ andata e ritorno*
airport	*aeroporto*		
train	*treno*	...first/second class	*....prima/seconda classe*
..station	*....stazione ferroviaria*	ticket office	*biglietteria*
bus	*autobus*	timetable	*orario*
..station	*....autostazione*	seat	*posto*
ferry	*traghetto*	non-smoking	*vietato fumaro*
ticket	*biglietto*	reserved	*prenotato*

yes	*sì*	help!	*aiuto!*
no	*no*	today	*oggi*
please	*per favore*	tomorrow	*domani*
thank you	*grazie*	yesterday	*ieri*
hello	*ciao*	how much?	*quanto?*
goodbye	*arrivederci*	expensive	*caro*
goodnight	*buona notte*	open	*aperto*
sorry	*mi dispiace*	closed	*chiuso*

INDEX

Acknowledgements
The Automobile Association wishes to thank the following libraries, photographers and associations for their assistance in the preparation of this book.

BRIDGEMAN ART LIBRARY/Vatican Museums and Galleries, Vatican City, Italy 24, 25, 27b; JOHN HESELTINE 90; MARY EVANS PICTURE LIBRARY 11,14; M R I BANKERS' GUIDE TO FOREIGN CURRENCY 119; SPECTRUM COLOUR LIBRARY 60, 89; THE STOCK MARKET, INC 27a; WORLD PICTURES LTD 12/3, 87.

The remaining transparencies are held in the Association's own library (AA PHOTO LIBRARY) with contributions from: J Holmes F/cover (b) woman, (c) sculptured hand, (f) scooter, B/cover Romulus and Remus, 5a, 5b, 12, 16, 18, 26, 34, 35b, 39, 44, 47, 48, 49, 51a, 52, 55b, 57a, 57b, 59, 61, 65, 70, 72, 76; D Mitidieri F/cover (d) plaque, 7, 8a, 8b, 9a, 9b, 20, 23, 32, 35a, 36, 38, 42, 43, 56, 64, 66, 68, 69, 71, 74, 75a, 75b, 78a, 78b, 84a, 91a, 91b; C Sawyer F/cover (bottom) statue, 1,15b, 17, 21, 22, 31, 33, 41, 50a, 86, 117b; L B Smith 122a; T Souter F/cover (e) Swiss Guard, 40, 53, 82, 83, 84b, 88, 117a; P Wilson F/cover (a) Colosseum, (g) sculptured head, 2, 6, 15a, 19, 37, 45, 50b, 55a, 62, 77, 79.

Author's Acknowledgements
Jane Shaw wishes to thank Fiona Benson for expertise on churches, shops and hotels, Roberta Mitchell for expertise on restaurants and food and Sally Webb for expertise on museums and excursions.

The Automobile Association wishes to thank Marco De Pellegrin for his insight and invaluable assistance.

Contributors
Copy editor: Pat Pierce Verifier: Teresa Fisher Researcher (Practical Matters): Colin Follett
Indexer: Marie Lorimer Revision management: Outcrop Publishing Services, Cumbria

Dear Essential Traveller

Your comments, opinions and recommendations are very important to us. So please help us to improve our travel guides by taking a few minutes to complete this simple questionnaire.

You do not need a stamp (unless posted outside the UK). If you do not want to cut this page from your guide, then photocopy it or write your answers on a plain sheet of paper.

Send to: **The Editor, AA World Travel Guides, FREEPOST SCE 4598, Basingstoke RG21 4GY.**

Your recommendations...

We always encourage readers' recommendations for restaurants, nightlife or shopping – if your recommendation is used in the next edition of the guide, we will send you a *FREE* AA *Essential* **Guide** of your choice. Please state below the establishment name, location and your reasons for recommending it.

_____

_____

_____

_____

Please send me **AA *Essential*** _____

(*see list of titles inside the front cover*)

About this guide...

Which title did you buy?

AA *Essential* _____

Where did you buy it? _____

When? m m / y y

Why did you choose an AA *Essential* Guide? _____

_____

_____

_____

_____

Did this guide meet your expectations?

Exceeded ☐ Met all ☐ Met most ☐ Fell below ☐

Please give your reasons_____

_____

_____

_____

continued on next page...

Were there any aspects of this guide that you particularly liked? _____
_____
_____
_____

Is there anything we could have done better? _____
_____
_____
_____
_____

About you...

Name (*Mr/Mrs/Ms*) _____
  Address _____
_____
  _____ Postcode _____
  Daytime tel nos _____

Which age group are you in?
  Under 25 ☐   25–34 ☐   35–44 ☐   45–54 ☐   55–64 ☐   65+ ☐

How many trips do you make a year?
  Less than one ☐   One ☐   Two ☐   Three or more ☐

Are you an AA member? Yes ☐   No ☐

About your trip...

When did you book? _ _ / _ _   When did you travel? _ _ / _ _
How long did you stay? _____
Was it for business or leisure? _____
Did you buy any other travel guides for your trip?
  If yes, which ones? _____
_____

Thank you for taking the time to complete this questionnaire. Please send
  it to us as soon as possible, and remember, you do not need a stamp
  (*unless posted outside the UK*).

Happy Holidays!